PEMBROKESHIRE AND CARMARTHENSHIRE

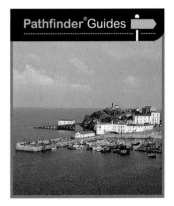

Pathfinder® Guides

Outstanding
Circular Walks

Revised by
Tom Hutton

Text:	Brian Conduit, Tom Hutton
Photography:	Crimson Publishing, Brian Conduit, Tom Hutton.
	Front cover: Dennis Kelsall
Editor:	Ark Creative (UK) Ltd
Designer:	Ark Creative (UK) Ltd

ISBN: 978-0-31909-037-4

While every care has been taken to ensure the accuracy of the route directions, the
publishers cannot accept responsibility for errors or omissions, or for changes in
details given. The countryside is not static: hedges and fences can be removed, field
boundaries can alter, stiles can be replaced by gates, footpaths can be rerouted and
changes in ownership can result in the closure or diversion of some concessionary
paths. Also, paths that are easy and pleasant for walking in fine conditions may
become slippery, muddy and difficult in wet weather, while stepping stones across
rivers and streams may become impassable.

If you find an inaccuracy in either the text or maps, please write to Crimson
Publishing at the address below.

First published 1993 by Jarrold Publishing
Revised and reprinted 1996, 1998, 2004, 2007

This edition first published in Great Britain 2010 by Crimson Publishing and
reprinted with amendments in 2014, 2017 and 2019.

Crimson Publishing, 19-21C Charles Street, Bath, BA1 1HX

www.pathfinderwalks.co.uk

Printed in India by Replika Press Pvt. Ltd. 13/19

A catalogue record for this book is available from the British Library.

Front cover: Pwll Gwylog towards Dinas Island
Previous page: Tenby

Contents

Approximate walk times

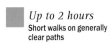 *Up to 2 hours*
Short walks on generally clear paths

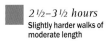 *2½–3½ hours*
Slightly harder walks of moderate length

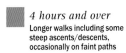 *4 hours and over*
Longer walks including some steep ascents/descents, occasionally on faint paths

The walk times are provided as a guide only and are calculated using an average walking speed of 2½mph (4km/h), adding one minute for each 10m (33ft) of ascent, and then rounding the result to the nearest half hour.

Walks are considered to be dog friendly unless specified.

Keymap 1

SCALE 1:250 000 or 1 INCH to 4 MILES *1CM to 2.5KM*

KILOMETRES

MILES

KEYMAP HEIGHTS SHOWN IN METRES

PEMBROKESHIRE COAST
NATIONAL PARK/
PARC CENEDLAETHOL
ARFORDIR PENFRO

Keymap 1

Pwllygranant

Y Ferwig

CARDIGAN/
ABERTEIFI
Bridgend

Penparc
Tremain

St Dogmaels
Abbey
Moylgrove
Monington
Glanrhyd
Pen-y-pryn
Bridell
Llantood
Rhos-Hill

Llangoedmor
Llechryd
Cilgerran
Castle
Cilgerran
Newchapel
Abercych
Boncath
Blaenffos
Bwlchygroes
Star

Capel Tygw
Llandygw

DINAS HEAD
8

Brynhenllan
Dinas
Cross
Newport
Nevern
Carreg
Coetan
Parrog

Felindre
Farchog
A487
Afon
Nyfer
9

Crosswell
Eglwyswen
Eglwyswrw
Llanfair-
Nant-Gwyn

Frenni Fawr
395

Crymych
Hermon
Llanfyrnach
Tegryn

Fishguard/
Abergwaun

Mynydd Melyn
307
Cilgwyn
Pontfaen
24

Mynydd Carningli
311

Brynberian

MYNYDD PRESELI
Foel Eryr
468
536
28

Mynachlog-ddu
Foel-drych
Pentre Galar
Glandwr
Glandwr
Blaenwaun

Rosebush
Castlebythe
Little Newcastle
Tufton
Henry's
Moat
Ambleston
Wallis
Rinaston
Spittal
Walton
East
Scolton

Maenclochog
Dandderwen
Llanglolman
Glandy
Cross
Efailwen
Cefn-y-pant
Hebron
Llanglydwen
Cwmfelin
Mynach
Llanboidy

New Moat
Llys-y-frân
Penffordd
Llanycefn
Login
Crosshands
Clarbeston
Clarbeston
Road
Bletherston
Llandissilio
Hiraeth
Henllan
Amgoed
Llangynin

Crundale
Wiston
Gelli
Bethesda
16
Castle
Clunderwen
Llanfallteg
Rhydwyrach
Cwmfelin
Boeth

HAVERFORDWEST/
HWLFFORDD
Uzmaston
Llawhaden
Robeston
Wathen
A40
Narberth Station
Llanddewi
Velfrey
Whitland
Trevaughan
Llwyn-y-brain
Llanddowror

The Rhos
Picton
Castle
Minwear
NARBERTH
Crinow
Lampeter
Velfrey
Tavernspite
Red Roses
Llandawke
Llansadurnen

Boulston
Landshipping
Martletwy
A4075
Cold Blow
Templeton
Princes Gate
Ludchurch
Llanteg
Marros
Pendine

New Park
Yerbeston
Thomas
Chapel
Reynalton
11
Mountain
Houghton
Burton
Lawrenny
Cresswell
Quay
Jeffreyston
Loveston
Begelly
Broadmoor
Kilgetty
Stepaside
Amroth
Pendine San

West
Williamston
Carew
Newton
Cresselly
Pentlepoir
Wooden
Saundersfoot

Coshestone
Milton
Carew
Cheriton
Sageston
East
Williamston
Monkstone
Point

PEMBROKE
Lamphey
Manorbier
Newton
St Florence
Gumfreston
12
TENBY/
DINBYCH-Y-PYSGOD

Cheriton or
Stackpole Elidor
Hodgeston
Jameston
Penally
Giltar
Point
CARMARTHEN BAY/
BAE CAERFYRDDIN

Stackpole
Freshwater
East
Trewent
Point
Manorbier
Castle
2
Old Castle
Head
Caldey Island/
Ynys Bŷr
Monastery
Chapel
Point

27
Stackpole
Head
Barafundle Bay
Caldey Sound

Tan-y-groes
Glynarthen
Rhydlewis
Capel Cynon
Gwardafolog
Bwlch-y-fadfa
Aber
Cwrtnewydd
Llanwnnen
Blaenporth
Betws Ifan
Troedyraur
Penrhiw-pal
Flostrasol
Moel y Môr
Pont-Siân
Rhydowen
Llanwenog
Cwmsychbant
Dre-fach
Alltyblaca
Llanybydder

Ponthirwaun
Bryngwyn
Brongest
Penrhiw-llan
Croes-lan
Tregroes
Prengwyn
Capel Dewi
Maesycrugiau
Aber-Giâr

Cenarth
Cwm-cou
Llandyfriog
Aber-banc
Maes llyn
Horeb
Llandysul
Llanfihangel-ar-arth
Llanllwni

NEWCASTLE EMLYN
A484
Pentrecagal
Henllan
Llangeler
Pont Tyweli
Gwarallt
Gwndwn
Penrherber
Drefach
Felindre
Pentre-cwrt
Bancyffordd
Pencader
New Inn
A485

Capel Iwan
Drefelin
Saron
Cwmpengraig
Rhos
Dolgran
Gwyddgrug

Cilrhedyn
Cwmorgan
Moeltre
Cwmduad
Alltwalis
Brechfa

Dinas
Bryn Iwan
Hermon
Llanpumsaint
Llanllawddog
Horeb

Trelech
Esgair
Cynwyl Elfed
Pontarsais
Plas Fawr

Pen-y-bont
Blaen-y-coed
Rhydargaeau
Llanwinio
Talog
Pentre-Morgan
A485

Gellywen
Bwlchnewydd
Abernant
Newchurch
Bronwydd Arms
Llanfihangel uwch-Gwili

Meidrim
Merthyr
Ffynnon-ddrain
ROMAN AMPHITHEATRE
Capel Gwyn
Nantgaredig

CARMARTHEN / CAERFYRDDIN
Llangunnor
Abergwili
Capel Dewi
Llanarthne

Bancyfelin
Llanllwch
Nantycaws
A48

St Clears / Sanclêr
Llangynog
Llangain
Cwmffrwd
Croesyceiliog
Cwmisfael
Porthyrhyd
Llanddarog

Motte & Bailey
Morfa Bach
Llangyndeyrn
Pontantwn
Crwbin
Pontyberem
Meinciau
Tumble

Llandawke
Llansadurnen
Llansteffan
Llanybri
Llandyfaelog
Ferryside
Pontyates
Pont Henri
Llannon
Sylen

Laugharne
Broadway
Broadlay
Llansaint
Broadway
KIDWELLY
Mynyddygarreg
Cynheidre
Five Roads
Carway
Trimsaran
Pen-y-mynydd
Felinfoel

Brook
Llanmiloe
East Marsh
Pendine
Ginst Point
St Ishmael
Pendine Sands
Laugharne Sands

Cefn Sidan Sands
Pembrey Forest
Mynydd Pen-bre
BURRY PORT
Pwll
Dafen

CARMARTHEN BAY / BAE CAERFYRDDIN
Pembrey
Cefn Padrig
LLANELLI
Llwynhendy

Whiteford Point
Llanrhidian Sands
Crofty

At-a-glance

Walk	Page	Start	Nat. Grid Reference	Distance	Time	Height Gain
Angle Point & West Angle Bay	77	West Angle Bay	SM 854031	9 miles (14.5km)	4½ hrs	1,195ft (365m)
Blacktar Point, Llangwm and Benton Wood	36	Blacktar Point	SM 998095	4½ miles (7.2km)	2½ hrs	560ft (170m)
Bosherston Lily Ponds & The Green Bridge of Wales	85	Bosherston	SR 967948	10 miles (16.1km)	5 hrs	820ft (250m)
Brechfa Forest	34	Brechfa village	SN 524302	4 miles (6.4km)	2½ hrs	820ft (250m)
Broad Haven and Haroldston Wood	26	Broad Haven	SM 863140	4 miles (6.4km)	1½ hrs	395ft (120m)
Carew	14	Carew Castle	SN 046036	2 miles (3.2km)	1 hr	165ft (50m)
Cilgerran & the Teifi gorge	53	Cilgerran Coracle Centre	SN 197429	6 miles (9.7km)	3 hrs	870ft (265m)
Dale Peninsula	56	Dale	SM 811058	6½ miles (10.4km)	3 hrs	590ft (180m)
Dinas Island	30	Pwllgwaelod	SN 005398	3 miles (4.8km)	1½ hrs	655ft (200m)
Goodwick and Carregwastad Point	44	Goodwick	SM 949390	5 miles (8km)	2½ hrs	755ft (230m)
Gwaun Valley and Carningli	74	Pontfaen	SN 024339	8 miles (12.9km)	4 hrs	1,180ft (360m)
Laugharne and the Taf Estuary	58	Laugharne	SN 301106	6½ miles (10.5km)	3 hrs	770ft (235m)
Llandeilo and Dinefwr Park	20	Llandeilo	SN 629222	3 miles (4.8km)	1½ hrs	425ft (130m)
Llansteffan and the Towy Estuary	23	Llansteffan	SN 355108	3¼ miles (5.2km)	1½ hrs	395ft (120m)
Llawhaden and the Eastern Cleddau	50	Llawhaden	SN 070173	5½ miles (8.8km)	3 hrs	720ft (220m)
Manorbier	16	Manorbier	SS 063976	2 miles (3.2km)	1½ hrs	490ft (150m)
Newcastle Emlyn and Cenarth	64	Newcastle Emlyn	SN 309407	6½ miles (10.5km)	3½ hrs	1,015ft (310m)
Pentre Ifan	32	Pentre Ifan Farm	SN 092383	4 miles (6.5km)	2 hrs	590ft (180m)
The Preseli Ridge	89	Bwlch-gwynt	SN 074321	10½ miles (16.9km)	5 hrs	1,510ft (460m)
Porthgain & Abereiddi	28	Porthgain	SM 815325	3½ miles (5.6km)	2 hrs	260ft (80m)
Saundersfoot & Tenby	39	Saundersfoot	SN 136048	4 miles (6.5km)	2½ hrs	1,085ft (330m)
Solva & Pointz Castle	47	Solva	SM 805243	5 miles (8km)	3 hrs	855ft (260m)
St David's Head and Carn Llidi	42	Whitesands Bay	SM 734271	4½ miles (7.2km)	2½ hrs	935ft (285m)
St David's, Porth Clais and Ramsey Sound	81	St David's	SM 757252	9 miles (14.5km)	4½ hrs	770ft (235m)
St Non's and Caerfai	18	St David's	SM 757252	3½ miles (5.6km)	2 hrs	395ft (120m)
Strumble Head	61	Garn Fawr	SM 898388	6¾ miles (10.8km)	3½ hrs	1,295ft (395m)
Treffgarne gorge and mountain	67	Nant-y-Coy Mill	SM 956252	7 miles (11.3km)	3½ hrs	835ft (255m)
Wooltack Point and Marloes	71	Martin's Haven	SM 760089	7 miles (11.3km)	4 hrs	425ft (130m)

Comments

A demanding yet enthralling ramble around an ever-changing section of coastline where the tranquil inland waters of Milford Haven meet the roaring surf of the Atlantic.

From many points on the walk there are fine views across the wide estuary of the Daugleddau, the upper reaches of Milford Haven.

A grand coastal walk is combined with the attractive lily ponds at Bosherston and the tiny, 13th-century St Govan's Chapel.

A lovely ramble through fine deciduous woodland and alongside the sylvan Afon Cothi. Finishes by climbing high onto the open hillside and following easy lanes.

An attractive combination of woodland and coastal walking, with a final stretch above a glorious sandy beach.

A short walk, mostly across meadows bordering the Daugleddau, which passes an ancient cross and visits the impressive Carew Castle and Mill.

At the end of the walk comes the dramatic scene of the towers of Cilgerran Castle rising above the thickly wooded Teifi Gorge.

Apart from a short opening inland stretch, the whole of the walk follows the coast path around the Dale Peninsula, which juts out into the entrance to Milford Haven.

Some splendid cliff scenery can be enjoyed on this easy, though spectacular walk around the peninsula of Dinas Island.

This is a fairly energetic walk to the east of Fishguard harbour, which gives extensive views both along the coast and inland to the Preseli Hills.

The first and last parts of the route are through the remote and thickly wooded Gwaun Valley. In contrast, the middle section is over the open moorland of Carningli.

The ingredients of this fine and varied walk include woodland, marshland, estuary, attractive town, church, ruined castle and plenty of reminders of Dylan Thomas.

This walk through attractive parkland gives you superb views over the Vale of Towy and passes the ruins of a medieval castle and a 17th-century house.

Llansteffan Castle is in sight for much of the way, there is attractive walking beside the estuary and the magnificent views extend across to Gower.

A most attractive walk, mainly through woodlands and across meadows on both banks of the Eastern Cleddau, with an interesting medieval church and castle.

A grand walk along the coastal path leads back to the sandy beach at Manorbier, flanked by the twin medieval buildings of castle and church.

As well as grand views over the Teifi Valley, there are castle remains at Newcastle Emlyn and the impressive falls and dramatic wooded gorge at Cenarth.

A fine, varied walk through deciduous woodland and over a lofty, rock-topped heath. The return leg passes an impressive prehistoric burial chamber.

This is a there-and-back walk along an ancient route across the bare moorland expanses of the Preseli Hills. There are extensive views and a number of prehistoric sites.

Two enchanting historic ports linked by one of the most rugged yet beautiful sections of the coast path. An easy return leg follows farm tracks over open hillside.

A linear coastal walk between the two biggest resorts on the South Pembrokeshire coast. Includes a visit to a very secluded beach.

There is splendid cliff walking and grand views, especially on the final descent above Solva's picturesque harbour.

The walk takes you from the wide beach at Whitesands Bay, around St David's Head and up to the summit of Carn Llidi. From here the views are magnificent.

One of the finest coastal walks in the country has the considerable historic appeal and superb collection of medieval monuments of St David's as an added bonus.

This is the easiest coastal walk in the St David's area but it follows a stunning section of coastline and also pays a visit to the birthplace of the patron saint.

Starting from an Iron Age fort, this walk takes you along one of the wildest and loneliest parts of the Pembrokeshire coast.

Do not be misled by the name Great Treffgarne Mountain; the climb over its bare slopes from the thickly wooded Treffgarne gorge is easy and gradual.

Some of the finest beaches on the Pembrokeshire coast are passed on this magnificent walk around the Marloes Peninsula, on the south side of St Bride's Bay.

Introduction to Pembrokeshire and Carmarthenshire

Although neighbours, Pembrokeshire and Carmarthenshire have their own individual characteristics. Pembrokeshire has a strong English influence, evident in the place names in the southern half of the county and the distinctive, tall and often crenellated English-style towers of many of the churches. In contrast, Carmarthenshire is a bastion of Welsh culture and language.

At the same time, these two counties of West Wales share some common features. They were both part of the ancient Welsh kingdom of Deheubarth and possess numerous ruined castles. Both have much superb, varied and unspoilt countryside that makes them a paradise for walkers. Pembrokeshire has some of the most spectacular coastal scenery and finest stretches of coast path in Britain. Carmarthenshire is noted for its rolling hills, wide river valleys and a coastline of long sandy beaches fringing Carmarthen Bay, broken into by the combined estuaries of the Gwendraeth, Towy and Taf rivers. Due to the obvious attraction for walkers of the Pembrokeshire Coast National Park, Pembrokeshire accounts for 23 of the 28 walks in this guide.

Pembrokeshire

The Pembrokeshire Coast National Park was created in 1952. It is the smallest of the ten original national parks of England and Wales and unique in that it is the only one based on a coastline rather than on predominantly mountain or moorland regions. For the most part it comprises a narrow strip of land stretching along the whole length of the Pembrokeshire coast with just two breaks: a short one around Fishguard harbour and a longer one around the industrial zone that fringes Milford Haven.

Rugged and lonely, sometimes calm and gentle, and at other times pounded by waves and westerly gales, few would dispute that the Pembrokeshire coast is one of the most magnificent in the country. For such a relatively small area the geological structure is complex and unusually diverse, the area having some of the oldest rocks in Britain. In general, the older rocks are in the north, where the many bold headlands and outcrops, such as Strumble Head and Carn Llidi, represent intrusions of harder and more resistant rocks. The younger rocks are in the south, chiefly old red sandstone and carboniferous limestone, the latter especially noticeable along the coast of the Castlemartin peninsula.

A glance at the map reveals that the Pembrokeshire coastline is heavily indented with a whole succession of both large and small headlands, peninsulas, bays and offshore islands, with some outstanding sandy beaches. The Pembrokeshire Coast Path, opened in 1970, follows all these indentations, making it more than 180 miles (290km) long. Walking it is a sheer delight, particularly in spring and early summer, when the weather is more settled and the profusion of wild flowers further enhances the surrounding cliff scenery.

Although mainly coastal, the national park boundaries in two instances reach inland to include two widely contrasting areas. In the south they extend along

the shores of the Daugleddau, the upper reaches of Milford Haven, formed by the combined estuaries of the Eastern and Western Cleddau, Carew and Cresswell rivers. This is a landscape of low-lying wooded shorelines, creeks and mudflats that is like no other in Pembrokeshire. In the north, the national park broadens out to include the Preseli Hills, whose

The Western Cleddau flows peacefully through Treffgarne gorge

open, windswept, lonely moorlands, despite rising to a maximum height of only 1,760ft (536m), dominate the surrounding countryside and provide outstanding views. A walk along the Preseli ridge is a most exhilarating experience, and different but equally rewarding is a walk through the superb woodlands of the Gwaun valley, which lie at the foot of the main ridge and separate it from the Carningli range to the north.

There is more to the region, however, than the national park. Much of inland Pembrokeshire lies outside its boundaries and, although the scenery may be less exciting, pleasant and interesting walking may be enjoyed in the valleys of the Eastern and Western Cleddau. Even here dramatic landscapes can be seen, as in the Treffgarne gorge, where the Western Cleddau squeezes between steep-sided cliffs below the conspicuous outcrops of Maiden Castle and Poll Carn, and in the Teifi gorge, where walkers can admire the striking view of the towers of Cilgerran Castle perched above the thickly wooded valley sides that inspired paintings by Wilson, Turner and others.

No walker in Pembrokeshire can fail to be aware of its past, especially the numerous prehistoric remains and medieval castles and the region's associations with the early history of Christianity in Britain. From the prehistoric era came its cromlechs or burial chambers, the most impressive of which is Pentre Ifan, and its standing-stones, hut circles and Iron Age forts. Such remains are heavily concentrated on the Preseli Hills and neighbouring Carningli, and it was from these hills that the bluestones used in the construction of Stonehenge originated. Debate continues as to how the stones reached Salisbury Plain; were they erratic boulders carried by glacial ice or quarried and transported over land and water by Neolithic man? More certain is the fact that the Preseli ridge was part of an ancient routeway linking southern England, Wales and Ireland.

For those whose main impression of Pembrokeshire is of remoteness, it comes as a surprise to learn that in the Dark Ages this south-western tip of Wales was a centre of the Celtic world and at the crossroads of land and sea routes between Wales, Ireland, Cornwall and Brittany. St David's, bastion of early Celtic Christianity, major evangelising centre and holy city of Wales, is a fascinating and

Introduction

Introduction

still powerfully evocative spot. When Francis Kilvert came here in 1871 he wrote in his diary: 'And so we came to the end of the world where the Patron Saint of Wales sleeps by the western sea.'

Almost as evocative are the great castles that are scattered throughout the region, mostly founded by the Normans as they advanced along the southern coast of Wales. Most imposing of these is Pembroke, launch pad for the Norman invasion of Ireland and later the birthplace of Henry VII.

The Norman conquerors also introduced English and Flemish settlers into the southern half of Pembrokeshire, thus creating the cultural division between the predominantly Welsh-speaking north and the English-speaking south, the latter sometimes known as 'Little England beyond Wales'. The Landsker is the unofficial but clearly traced frontier between the two: to the north of it place-names are mainly Welsh and it has small, plain churches with bell-cotes; to the south of it place-names are English and the churches have tall, narrow, crenellated western towers.

Despite its isolation, Pembrokeshire has figured in at least two events of major national importance. In 1485 Henry Tudor landed on the shores of Milford Haven to begin the campaign that was to lead to his victory over Richard III and his accession to the throne as Henry VII. Further north, the last invasion of Britain occurred in 1797 when a French force landed on the coast near Fishguard during the Napoleonic Wars.

Modern transport developments have broken down much of Pembrokeshire's earlier isolation, and it has become a popular holiday destination. But the resorts have remained relatively small and unspoilt – even Tenby, the largest of them, can hardly rank with Blackpool or Bournemouth – there have been no really large-scale developments apart from the power station and oil-refining industries around Milford Haven, and the region still retains some of its character as a *gwlad hud a lledrith* 'land of magic and enchantment' as the ancients called it.

Carmarthenshire

Carmarthenshire is a large county and, apart from where the South Wales coalfield intruded into its south-eastern fringes, it has always been thinly-populated and mainly rural, with a large emphasis on sheep and dairy farming.

The historic county town of Carmarthen stands just above where the River Towy widens out into an estuary. North-eastwards the meandering river flows through a broad, lush and verdant vale, the county's chief physical feature, passing by the small market towns of Llandeilo and Llandovery and with the landscape punctuated by the ruins of medieval castles. The part of the county to the east of the Towy valley falls within the boundaries of the Brecon Beacons National Park but this area is covered by the *Brecon Beacons* Pathfinder® guide. Apart from the Towy, the only other river of any size is the Teifi, which flows through another broad vale and forms the county's northern border with Ceredigion.

Sandwiched between the cliffs, coves and glorious beaches of Pembrokeshire and Gower, the coastline of Carmarthenshire tends to get overlooked but the sands at Cefn Sidan near Pembrey and Pendine are some of the longest and finest in the country and in the years between the First and Second World Wars, the latter were famous as the setting for Sir Malcolm Campbell's attempts on the world land speed record. Perhaps the most striking feature of the Carmarthenshire coast is the wide, tree-fringed estuary formed by the Gwendraeth, Towy and Taf. Each river has its castle. Greatest of these is the magnificent castle at Kidwelly on the Gwendraeth but Llansteffan Castle dominates a wooded cliff above the Towy and the more homely castle

Fishguard harbour

at Laugharne lies beside the estuary of the Taf.

Laugharne's main claim to fame is that it was the home of Dylan Thomas. The turbulent poet writes that he 'got off the bus and forgot to get on again', because he liked the place so much and decided to settle there. Even allowing for artistic licence, you will begin to understand why after visiting this small town and sampling the countryside around it, featured in Walk 19.

Walking in the area

In a walking guide to Pembrokeshire and Carmarthenshire there is an inevitable concentration on coastal walking, especially using the Pembrokeshire Coast Path, which is well-waymarked and easy to follow. On the Pembrokeshire coast the many headlands and small peninsulas allow circular routes that keep almost entirely to the coast, with just a brief inland section across the neck of the headland.

The coasts of Pembrokeshire and Carmarthenshire present few of the potential dangers of mountain walking in places such as Snowdonia, the Lake District or Scotland, and few of the navigational hazards that may be encountered in featureless moorland areas like Dartmoor or Yorkshire. It is important, however, to keep a look out for bad weather and in particular to avoid coastal walking in strong winds; battling along an exposed coast path during a gale can be extremely hazardous and the dangers should not be underestimated.

In fine conditions, whether enjoying the dramatic surroundings of the coast paths or sampling the variety of landscape found inland, walking in Pembrokeshire and Carmarthenshire is a most rewarding experience, not least because of the sense of isolation and awareness of the past that both counties share.

This book includes a list of waypoints alongside the description of the walk, so that you can enjoy the full benefits of gps should you wish to. For more information on using your gps, read the *Pathfinder® Guide GPS for Walkers,* by gps teacher and navigation trainer, Clive Thomas (ISBN 978-0-7117-4445-5). For essential information on map reading and basic navigation, read the *Pathfinder® Guide Map Reading Skills* by outdoor writer, Terry Marsh (ISBN 978-0-7117-4978-8). Both titles are available in bookshops or can be ordered online at www.pathfinderwalks.co.uk

Introduction

Carew

Start	Carew Castle	GPS waypoints
Distance	2 miles (3.2km)	☑ SN 046 036
Height gain	165 feet (50m)	Ⓐ SN 042 039
		Ⓑ SN 045 045
Approximate time	1 hour	Ⓒ SN 042 046
Parking	Car park at Carew Castle	Ⓓ SN 045 039
Route terrain	Well-waymarked footpaths along the edge of the Mill Pond and across fields	
Ordnance Survey maps	Landranger 158 (Tenby & Pembroke), Explorer OL36 (South Pembrokeshire)	

A remarkable variety of historic interest is crammed into this short and easy stroll, mostly across flat meadowland, in the low-lying country of the Daugleddau, the upper reaches of Milford Haven. The attractions include a mainly medieval castle, an 18th-century mill and an 11th-century cross. The walk as described makes a figure of eight to maximise the views. It could be shortened to a circuit around the mill pond if preferable.

For most of this walk there is a superb view across the waters of the Mill Pond to the ruins of Carew Castle. This dates mainly from the 13th and 14th centuries, but in the late 16th century Sir John Perrot, Lord Deputy of Ireland, who was granted the castle by Elizabeth I, built the impressive north gallery, transforming Carew into a harmonious combination of medieval fortress and Elizabethan manor house.

🗹 Exit the car park towards the castle ruins and turn left onto the lane. Now follow it easily along with great views of the castle until you reach a fork. Keep right and you'll soon reach the French Mill, so called because its millstones came from France. Although there has been a mill here since at least the 16th century, the present building dates from the late 18th century with 19th century additions and has been recently restored. It used the

Carew Castle across the waters of the Mill Pond

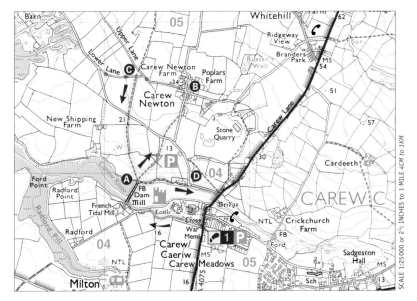

SCALE 1:25000 or 2½ INCHES to 1 MILE 4CM to 1KM

energy of the tides to drive the machinery and is the only remaining example of a tidal mill left in Wales.

Turn right along a path that leads over the dam and at the far side, go up steps and cross a stile next to a bench **A**. The path forks here so take the right-hand fork and follow it up towards the top right-hand corner. Go through a gate and keep ahead, with the hedge to your left to another gate that leads onto a lane. Cross the lane and go through a gate opposite to continue in the same direction to a stile. Cross this and turn left to walk up the lane towards the village of Carew Newton. Turn left at the top of the hill **B** and follow the lane easily out of the village, with great views down over the valley.

The lane bends right and then forks, take the left fork, and then, after 20 yds, at a footpath waymark, turn left over a stone stile into a field **C**. Now keep straight ahead, with the hedge to your left, to another stile and cross this onto a lane.

Keep straight across, over another stile, and continue in the same direction to yet another stone stile. Cross this and continue down with the hedge to your left to another stile, then go over this and keep straight ahead, now with wonderful views down over the mill and the castle. Continue down to the stile you crossed earlier at **A** and cross it again. Now turn left to follow a well-surfaced path along the edge of the Mill Pond, keeping below a car park and picnic area and eventually joining a lane **D**. Keep straight along the lane ahead to the main road and turn right to cross the bridge with care and walk up past the **Carew Inn**. Opposite this, by a barrier on the right, bear right into the castle grounds. Now explore both the castle and the 11th-century cross at will. The cross commemorates Meredudd ap Edwin, joint ruler of Deneubarth, a kingdom that covered south-west Wales, who was killed in battle in 1035. The elaborate patterns carved on this 13 foot-high monument are chiefly Celtic but have some Viking influence. An exit leads back onto the lane by the car park.

Manorbier

		GPS waypoints
Start	Manorbier	☑ SS 063 976
Distance	2 miles (3.2km)	Ⓐ SS 069 970
Height gain	490 feet (150m)	Ⓑ SS 070 976
Approximate time	1½ hours	Ⓒ SS 066 978
Parking	Pay and Display car park behind the beach	
Route terrain	Coast path, field paths and narrow lanes	
Dog friendly	Some awkward stiles; livestock. Scoop poop on beach	
Ordnance Survey maps	Landranger 158 (Tenby & Pembroke), Explorer OL36 (South Pembrokeshire)	

The medieval Welsh churchman Giraldus Cambrensis, who was born at Manorbier in 1146, described the village as 'the pleasantest spot in Wales'. Walkers can judge this for themselves on this ramble that takes in a short and relatively easy section of the coast path on the east of Manorbier Bay before returning, via field paths and tracks, to the village with its twin historic attractions of medieval church and castle.

At Manorbier the castle and church occupy opposite sides of a shallow valley that leads to a sandy bay. The substantial and well-preserved castle, a mainly late 13th- and early 14th century rebuilding of the original Norman structure, belonged to the de Barri family, whose most famous family member was Gerald de Barri, better known as Giraldus Cambrensis or Gerald of Wales. In 1188 he guided the

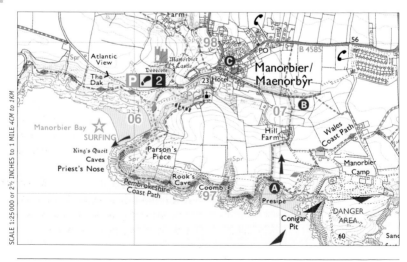

The medieval church at Manorbier

Archbishop of Canterbury on a tour around Wales to recruit volunteers for the crusade to the Holy Land, and his detailed accounts of this journey in *Itinerary through Wales and Description of Wales and its People* are invaluable historic sources, giving a fascinating insight into Welsh life at the time. Despite holding several important positions in the Church, Gerald never accomplished either of his two main ambitions: to create an independent Welsh Church and to become Bishop of St David's.

Manorbier church, dedicated to St. James the Greater, is also of Norman origin, with subsequent additions. Its irregularity gives it a highly distinctive appearance, and it has the usual tall, narrow, crenellated tower that is found in this part of Pembrokeshire.

Begin by taking the path at the far end of the car park, signposted 'Beach Access' which leads to the beach. Bear left to walk across the sand to a flight of steps at the far end by a coast path sign. Climb the steps and then a stile and follow the coast path to the end of the headland. To the right is a fine view across Manorbier Bay, looking towards St Govan's Head.

Just before rounding the headland

you pass King's Quoit, a neolithic burial chamber. Continue along the coast path that winds across smooth, sloping, grassy cliffs, passing some spectacular rock pinnacles. After going through a gate at a footpath sign, turn left **A** away from the coast and head gently uphill along the left-hand edge of a field, at first by a wall and later by a wire fence on the left. Continue to a small copse where a waymark post directs diagonally right to a stile. Cross this and follow the grassy track past Hill Farm. As the track swings left, keep ahead to cross a stile and then keep straight ahead across the field to aim for a waymarker by a telegraph pole. Go through a gap in the wall and descend to a stile and footpath sign. Climb the stile, descend some stone steps and continue downhill across a field, veering slightly left to pass through a wall gap. Turn left **B**, climb a stile and walk along a track, passing to the left of a house. Ahead the tall, narrow tower of Manorbier church can be seen.

At a T-junction of tracks bear right to continue along a hedge-lined track, eventually passing between houses to reach the road in Manorbier village. Turn left **C**, following signs to 'Car park, beach and castle', along a road that returns directly to the starting point.

If you wish to visit the church, take the first turning on the left and follow a narrow lane that descends, turns sharply right and then heads uphill. Where it curves left just before reaching the church, a path leads off to the right and heads down into the car park. ●

St Non's and Caerfai

Start	St David's	
Distance	3½ miles (5.6km)	
Height gain	395 feet (120m)	
Approximate time	2 hours	
Parking	St David's main car park	
Route terrain	Coast path, footpaths and farm tracks prone to mud	
Dog friendly	Best on lead around St Non's Chapel	
Ordnance Survey maps	Landranger 157 (St David's & Haverfordwest), Explorer OL35 (North Pembrokeshire)	

GPS waypoints

- ☑ SM 757 252
- Ⓐ SM 751 249
- Ⓑ SM 740 242
- Ⓒ SM 750 242
- Ⓓ SM 759 243

The coastline that loops around St David's is among the most stunning in the National Park but the path that follows this stretch is mainly rough and hilly and easy walks can be hard to come by. This short walk proves the exception, starting in St David's and joining the coast at the attractive little harbour of Porthclais. The going is scenic but generally very easy, and there's the added attraction of a visit to the ruins of a tiny chapel that marks the birthplace of St David. The final leg passes above the beautiful beach of Caerfai which is easily reached by a short detour.

The main car park in St David's is a little way east of the tiny city, next to the excellent tourist information centre.

St Non's Bay

☑ From the car park, turn left onto the road and walk towards Caerfai Bay. Ignore the first turning on the right at the top end of the car park but take the second, which leads into a residential

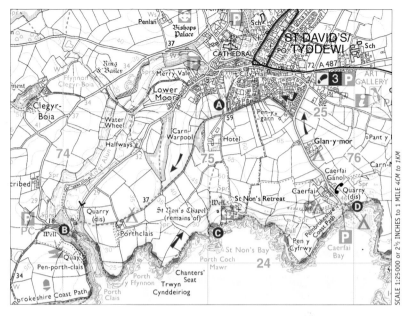

area, and then swing immediately left onto a waymarked hedged bridleway. Follow this past the end of another residential road to a junction with a lane Ⓐ.

Walk straight across this and take the waymarked path straight ahead to a fork. Keep right to cross a stile and then keep the hedge to your left to another stile, which you cross close to a farm. Go through the gate ahead and turn left towards the farm and then turn right. Then, as the drive swings left, bear right, keeping the hedge to your right, to walk through the caravan park to gorse bushes on the far side. Keep straight ahead to a path junction where you keep straight ahead to the road above Porthclais.

Turn left to drop to the bottom of the valley and then turn left again onto the coast path Ⓑ keeping the stream and bridge to your right. Climb up to the cliff tops, which offer great views over the harbour, and then veer around to the left with the views now over St. Bride's Bay. Follow the path easily around the inlet of Porth y Ffynnon and

continue past the headland of Trwyn Cynddeiriog and on towards St. Non's.

Keep your eye open for a footpath on the left Ⓒ that leads up to the ruined chapel, which marks the spot where legend suggests St David was born around AD500. Little is known about the life of the patron saint but it is thought he travelled extensively before finally returning to his birthplace to found a church and monastery close to the site of the present Cathedral. The location is named after his mother, St Non.

From the chapel head up to a gate that leads to the Holy Well. The well, which is actually shrouded by a grotto, is fed from a field spring which is said to have sprung up on the night of St David's birth. To return to the coast, pass beneath the new chapel to another gate. Turn left and continue easily around to Caerfai Bay. At the car park Ⓓ turn left to follow the lane back to St David's and the main car park, or continue down steps to the beach. ●

Llandeilo and Dinefwr Park

		GPS waypoints
Start	Llandeilo	🔎 SN 629 222
Distance	3 miles (4.8km)	**Ⓐ** SN 627 220
Height gain	425 feet (130m)	**Ⓑ** SN 611 217
Approximate time	1½ hours	**Ⓒ** SN 615 223
Parking	Llandeilo or street-side parking by the bridge near **Ⓐ**	**Ⓓ** SN 625 225
Route terrain	Woodland paths, field paths and a surfaced drive	
Ordnance Survey maps	Landranger 159 (Swansea & Gower), Explorer 186 (Llandeilo & Brechfa Forest)	

Most of this short walk is through the historic and highly attractive Dinefwr Park, a rolling, hilly area of parkland to the west of Llandeilo now owned by the National Trust. As well as outstanding views over the Towy Valley, the park has a ruined medieval castle and 17th-century mansion and is home to one of the few remaining breeds of White Park cattle. The route, which uses several of the well-waymarked, colour-coded trails created by the Trust, also passes by an ancient church.

The pleasant old market town of Llandeilo occupies the slopes of a hill overlooking the wide and fertile Vale of Towy.

🔎 Start in the main street by the church and facing it, turn right downhill to the bridge over the River Towy. Do not cross it but turn right **Ⓐ** along a lane beside the river and where it ends, keep ahead along an enclosed track to two gates. Go through the right-hand gate to the bottom edge of woodland and head gently uphill along a track, turn right through another gate to reach a fork.

Take the left-hand track, heading downhill and passing between gateposts to Llandyfeisant church. This old church stands on an ancient site and is the burial place for some members of the Rhys family of Dinefwr. Pass to the right of the church, walk along a path

to a gate, go through here entering Dinefwr Park, noted for its fine ancient oaks.

Keep left to walk along the left edge of the parkland. Go through a gate, bear left to go through another one and head up a wooded hillside (steps in places) to another gate. Go through, keep ahead to join a track and continue steadily uphill along it. Keep an eye open for a gate on the left and go through it to head up through trees, bushes and bracken to a T-junction, turn left to rejoin the track and follow it up to the remains of Dinefwr Castle **Ⓑ**.

For centuries the castle was the seat of the Rhys family, the ancient rulers of Deheubarth, a Welsh kingdom that covered most of south-west Wales. It is thought that the first structure was built in the late 9th century but the present ruins date mainly from the 12th century.

Dinefwr Castle

Some additions were made in the 17th century in order to create a more 'romantic' appearance. The views from

the castle over the Towy Valley are both extensive and magnificent.

Leave the castle by the same path as you arrived and continue past the junction where you joined the main track until you reach a path to the left, next to a seat. Take this and follow it down through woodland and out onto

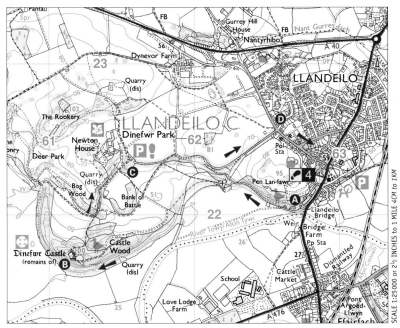

open ground, where you keep the woods to your right to drop straight downhill to a gate by a junction in the valley floor.

Newton House

Keep ahead through the gate, in the Newton House direction, walk along a track and go through another gate. The track passes to the left of a house, curves right and heads uphill, later becoming a tarmac track. On reaching a car park and visitor centre, **C** turn left for a brief detour to Newton House. This was built in the 17th century as a successor to the castle. The corner towers and cupolas were added in the 18th century and the whole building was refaced in limestone between 1856 and 1858. After many vicissitudes, the house has been restored by the National Trust and contains paintings and displays on the history of Dinefwr Park, plus a **café**.

Return to the car park **C** and turn left along the tarmac drive which winds through the park to emerge onto a road on the edge of Llandeilo **D**. Turn right and where the main road bends left, keep ahead into the town centre, descending to a T-junction. Turn right to return to the start. ●

Llandeilo Bridge

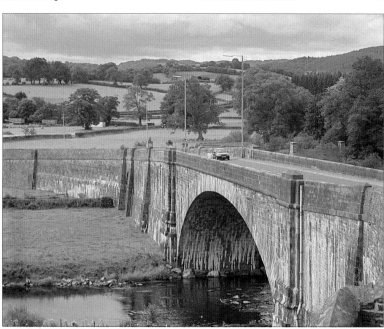

Llansteffan and the Towy Estuary

		GPS waypoints
Start	Llansteffan	SN 355 108
Distance	3¼ miles (5.2km)	Ⓐ SN 351 105
Height gain	395 feet (120m)	Ⓑ SN 346 098
Approximate time	1½ hours	Ⓒ SN 342 110
Parking	Beach car park	
Route terrain	Woodland paths and field paths, one steep climb	
Dog friendly	No dogs on main beach (May–September), some awkward stiles	
Ordnance Survey maps	Landranger 159 (Swansea & Gower), Explorer 177 (Carmarthen & Kidwelly)	

The first part of the walk is along the shore at the base of Llansteffan Castle. You continue below the castle walls to the lovely beach at Scott's Bay, then head up over a hill and descend back into Llansteffan. The castle is in sight for much of the way and from the higher points on the route, the superb views extend across Carmarthen Bay to Gower and Worms Head.

Whitewashed cottages overlook the sloping woodlands and sandy beaches of the Towy Estuary at Llansteffan and dominating this idyllic scene are the striking, hilltop ruins of the mainly 13th and 14th century castle, former residence of the local lords. Up in the village centre is the attractive medieval church, with a 13th century nave and 15th century tower.

There are two car parks near the beach and it does not really matter which you use; this route starts at the one farthest away from the castle.

Facing the estuary, turn right – either along a grassy path or along the edge of the beach – towards the castle and at the next car park, turn right across it to a waymarked post. Climb steps, head gently uphill along a fencelined path to a narrow lane and turn left Ⓐ. At a fork take the right-

Scott's bay near Llansteffan

Llansteffan Castle, Towy Estuary and Worms Head

hand lane then immediately, take the left-hand track through woodland. The track descends and where it ends at another fork, bear right along a wooded path that keeps above the estuary and below the castle walls.

At the next fork, take the left-hand path and descend steps to the sandy beach at Scott's Bay. Walk across it, go up a slipway and at a footpath post **B**, head directly uphill on an enclosed path through woodland to a gate. Go through, keep ahead along an enclosed track and go through another gate to a T-junction. Turn left, passing in front of a farmhouse, climb a stile and turn right uphill along the right edge of a field. Climb a stile in the top corner – from here the superb views take in Llansteffan Castle and extend across the bay to Worms Head on Gower – and keep ahead along the left edge of the next two fields to reach a lane.

Climb the stile opposite, walk along the left edge of a field, climb another stile and head gently uphill across the next field, making for a hedge corner. Just beyond it, climb a stile onto a lane **C**, turn left and almost immediately turn right over a stile, at a public footpath sign. Walk along an enclosed track, climb a stile, continue along the

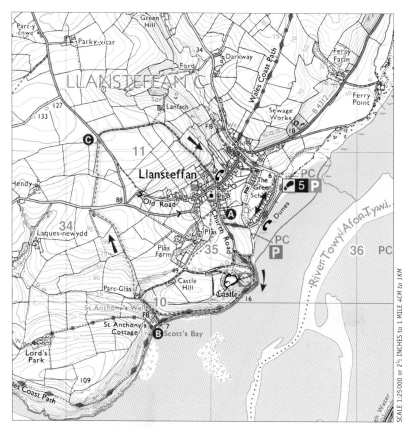

right edge of a field and after climbing another stile, bear right off the track and continue along the right field edge as the drive swings leftwards, directly above a farm, to a stile.

Climb it and with grand views ahead over the Towy Estuary, keep along the right edge of the next field, climb a stile and head gently downhill across a field to climb a stile in the bottom right-hand corner. Continue more steeply downhill along the right edge of the next field, climb a stile and head steeply down an enclosed wooded path to emerge onto a road in Llansteffan.

Take the road ahead – the church is to the right and there is a fine

view of the castle ahead – and look out for where you turn left **A** onto a descending path. Here you rejoin the outward route and retrace your steps to the start.

●

Llansteffan Castle

Broad Haven and Haroldston Wood

Broad Haven and Haroldston Wood

		GPS waypoints
Start	Broad Haven	📷 SM 863 140
Distance	4 miles (6.4km)	Ⓐ SM 864 148
Height gain	395 feet (120m)	Ⓑ SM 866 153
Approximate time	1½ hours	Ⓒ SM 867 158
Parking	Pay and Display car park behind the beach	Ⓓ SM 863 163
		Ⓔ SM 861 163
Route terrain	Woodland paths, coast path and a short section on a narrow lane	Ⓕ SM 861 140
Ordnance Survey maps	Landranger 157 (St David's & Haverfordwest), Explorer OL36 (South Pembrokeshire)	

The first half of the walk is mostly through lovely woodland and the second half is along the coast, descending into Broad Haven above the wide, sandy beach. This is an easy walk; the only steep climb is for those who opt for the higher of the two alternative paths through Haroldston Wood.

📷 Take the path that leads north out of the car park between the Youth Hostel and the Old Coastguard Station. Fork left at a junction with another path and continue to a kissing-gate. Cross a small footbridge to a junction with a

Broad Haven

path from the holiday park and turn half right, through a kissing-gate, to continue into the woods with the stream on your left. Continue over a footbridge, now with the stream to your right, and continue up through this narrow strip of lovely deciduous woodland on a clear path that eventually leads to a T-junction of paths by a tall fingerpost Ⓐ. Turn right to follow the clear path past a seat on your right, and then stay with it as it swings leftwards and continues to climb to another junction Ⓑ in front of St Madoc of Ferns' Church, the parish church for Haroldston West. Although on an ancient site, the present church was largely restored from ruins in 1883.

Ignore the direction of the footpath sign to the right and instead bear left and head up to climb a stile and keep ahead to a road. Bear right along the road, passing to the left of the church and keeping ahead at a junction in the direction of Nolton. After ¼ mile turn left **C** along a lane signposted to Druidston Haven and about ¼ mile after a sharp right-hand bend, at the

Haroldston Chin parking area **D**, turn left through a gate and walk along the right-hand edge of a field, by a wire fence on the right.

At the next coast path sign turn left **E** onto the coast path and follow it along the top of cliffs back to Broad Haven. This is an open and relatively easy section of the path which passes above some impressive cliffs before descending above the wide, flat sands of Broad Haven to a road **F**. Turn right along the road and after crossing a bridge over a narrow stream turn left along a tarmac path to return to the car park.

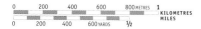

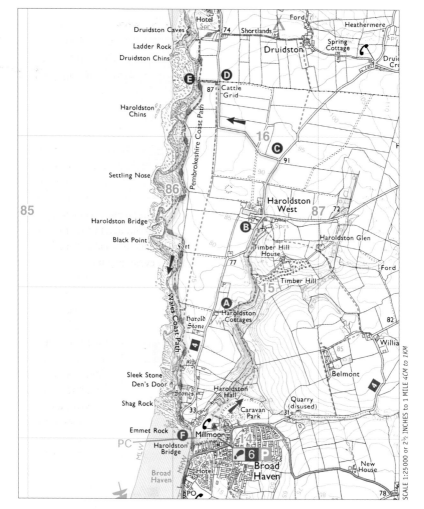

Porthgain and Abereiddi

		GPS waypoints
Start	Porthgain	
Distance	3½ miles (5.6km)	🥾 SM 815 325
Height gain	260 feet (80m)	Ⓐ SM 813 326
Approximate time	2 hours	Ⓑ SM 802 322
Parking	Porthgain (no charge)	Ⓒ SM 796 315
Route terrain	Coast path, footpaths and farm tracks prone to mud	Ⓓ SM 797 313
		Ⓔ SM 802 316
		Ⓕ SM 810 319
Ordnance Survey maps	Landranger 157 (St. David's & Haverfordwest), Explorer OL35 (North Pembrokeshire)	

This delightful strip of coastline has to be among the most scenic on the whole Pembrokeshire Coast Path. Porthgain is both quaint and fascinating in equal measures, and Abereiddi, with its turquoise pool, slate quarry ruins and gothic-looking folly offers plenty of opportunity for exploration. Between the two, there's a strip of typically rugged coast, broken up by a beautiful and often deserted beach.

It's amazing to think that the tiny village of Porthgain was once a thriving industrial centre, specialising in brick making and the quarrying and crushing of rock. But the evidence is definitely plain to see with the tall red brick ruins of the old storage hoppers towering above the quay, and there are further

Abereiddi Tower

ruined buildings up on the hill above the village, once connected by a tunnel.

🥾 To start the walk head down to the slipway in the main harbour wall and then bear left to walk in front of the **Shed Bistro** – an award-winning fish restaurant based in an old machine shop – to the far side of the quay. Turn right to walk along the far wall, now beneath the tumbledown storage hoppers, towards a small whitewashed building. Turn left Ⓐ beneath this building and climb steps all the way up onto the coast path.

Turn right to walk towards the coast with the sea to your right, and continue towards more ruined buildings where you'll easily make out the straight lines of a dismantled railway. Stay on the main path as it swings left, close to Porth Egr – a deep cleft in the cliffs with a fine beach beneath it, and continue to the next headland, where the path

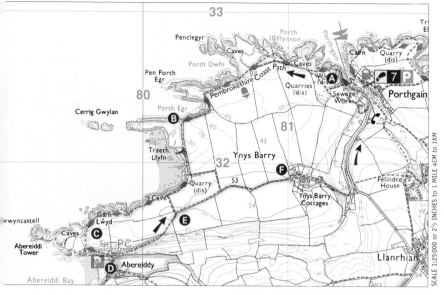

swings left again **B**.

Keep ahead now, passing steps that give easy and safe access to the beautiful and often deserted beach of Traeth Llyfn, and go through a gate at the top to bear around to the right, above the far end of the beach. The next headland, Carn Lwyd, offers wonderful views ahead to Trwyn Castell and Abereiddi Tower and the rocks on its summit make a great place to take a rest.

The tower was probably built as a navigation marker to guide boats looking for the quay, although some believe it may have been a folly built for quarry bosses' wives to enjoy afternoon tea. There are also signs of a much earlier promontory fort on the headland. To visit the tower, turn right off the path to drop into a steep-sided ravine and then scramble up the other side.

The coast path continues around to the left **C**, shortly offering fine views over the old quay and the eye-catching 'blue lagoon' – a stunning azure pool which was formed when the main slate quarry flooded in a storm in 1904.

Continue down towards the beach, where you'll see the remains of lime-kilns and worker's cottages, and keep left as the path bears right towards the beach **D** to go through a gate towards the public conveniences. Keep these to your left and go through another gate into a field. Keep to the left hand edge of the field, climbing steadily with gorse bushes to your left, and you'll cross the line of the old railway that once took slate from Abereiddi to Porthgain.

Continue to the top and cross a stile, then keep straight ahead to pass a wall corner to another stile **E**. Here, ignore a path that runs left back towards the coast and instead bear right to continue along the edge of the field, to another junction of paths where you take the broad farm track ahead.

This leads to Barry Island Farm **F**, where you keep straight ahead, keeping the farm buildings to the right. Continue along the drive and down into a dip, where you bear around to the left at a junction. This then climbs easily up to join the road, where you turn left to return to Porthgain. ●

Dinas Island

		GPS waypoints
Start	Pwllgwaelod. Turn off A487 at Dinas along lane to Bryn-henllan and Pwllgwaelod	☞ SN 005 398
Distance	3 miles (4.8km)	Ⓐ SN 005 411
Height gain	655 feet (200m)	Ⓑ SN 010 410
Approximate time	1½ hours	Ⓒ SN 014 401
Parking	Pwllgwaelod	
Route terrain	Coast path, field paths and easy track	
Dog friendly	No problems but scoop poop on beaches	
Ordnance Survey maps	Landrangers 145 (Cardigan & Mynydd Preseli) and 157 (St David's & Haverfordwest), Explorer OL35 (North Pembrokeshire)	

Cutting across the narrow neck of the peninsula of Dinas Island is a convenient short cut for those walking the Pembrokeshire Coast Path who want to reduce both distance and toil. But this walk shows that those who succumb to such temptation are missing out on a headland of great beauty, fine cliff scenery and ever-changing views, both inland and along the coast. Route finding could not be easier as you follow the well-waymarked coast path in a clockwise direction. Although a short walk, it is quite energetic with some reasonably steep ascents and descents.

As its name implies Dinas Island was once an island. At the end of the Ice Age, glacial meltwater scoured a channel across the neck of the peninsula linking Newport and Fishguard bays; that now dried-up channel forms the last part of the walk.

☞ Start by the **Old Sailors Restaurant** and walk towards the beach and then around to the right to the far end where you turn left to join the coast path. Now follow it around the headland, keeping the sea on the left all the while. The views are superb all the way: initially across Fishguard Bay as you climb to the triangulation pillar on Dinas Head (463feet/141m) Ⓐ, and

later, after rounding the head, over Newport Bay and inland to the line of the Preseli Hills on the skyline.

After passing above Pwll Glas you'll arrive at a gate Ⓑ. Pass through this and bear left to drop steeply down on a lovely, but narrow and quite exposed section of path. Follow this along, eventually crossing a shoulder with the sea stack of Needle Rock beneath you. This is an amazing place in spring, with a huge colony of guillemots and razorbills occupying every small ledge. You'll probably hear them before you see them.

Continue on the Coast Path, and you'll eventually start to drop south

A view from Dinas Head

towards Cwm-yr-Eglwys. The path winds easily down through woods, eventually emerging on a lane **C**.

Turn left into Cwm-yr-Eglwys, passing to the right of the ruined church, of which only the west wall and belfry remain. The 12th-century church, in a lovely position overlooking Newport Bay, was destroyed by a violent storm in 1859.

Take a footpath by public toilets on the right, keeping the boatyard to your left, and walk through a car park and onwards through a caravan site. This then turns to a pleasant tarmac path which crosses the neck of the peninsula, once covered by the sea.

Keep ahead, finally going through a kissing-gate close to the Old Sailors Restaurant and turning left to the car park at the starting point. ●

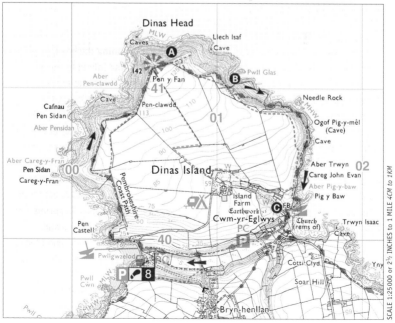

Pentre Ifan

		GPS waypoints
Start	Pentre Ifan Farm	☑ SN 092 383
Distance	4 miles (6.5km)	Ⓐ SN 093 376
Height gain	590 feet (180m)	Ⓑ SN 095 370
Approximate time	2 hours	Ⓒ SN 095 369
Parking	Small parking area at the entrance to Canolfan Pentre Ifan, south-west of Felindre Farchog	Ⓓ SN 090 366 / Ⓔ SN 092 359 / Ⓕ SN 101 370 / Ⓖ SN 101 375
Route terrain	Woodland paths, field paths, farm tracks and a quiet lane	
Ordnance Survey maps	Landranger 145 (Cardigan & Mynydd Preseli), Explorer OL35 (North Pembrokeshire)	

The main feature of this walk is the prehistoric burial chamber of Pentre Ifan, one of the finest in Wales and a superb vantage point overlooking Carningli and Cardigan Bay. The woodland of Tycanol Nature Reserve is delightful to walk through, and the highpoint of Carnedd Meibion-Owen offers even wider-ranging views over the ocean, Carningli and the nearby Preseli Hills.

☑ Leave the car park by walking down the drive towards Canolfan Pentre Ifan. Just ahead of the buildings, bear right onto a gravel track that then curves left, keeping the buildings to the left.

An exceptionally attractive part of the walk follows as the route continues

Carningli, framed by the impressive prehistoric burial chamber of Pentre Ifan

through the delightful Pentre-Evan Wood. Cross a stream, ignore a footpath on the left and continue past two turns to the right to a junction by a wall Ⓐ. Turn left and then right, through a gate, onto a sunken track. Now follow this (with a drive on your left) to another gate, where you bear half left onto a diverted section of footpath. Follow marker posts across the meadow and back into trees before emerging onto another meadow. Keep ahead, still following waymark posts, which eventually direct you back into the wood. Keep ahead through a muddy patch to a gate at the top Ⓑ.

Through the gate, head up the walled track all the way to a double gate Ⓒ, which leads you onto a lane. Turn right to a farm and then keep right to a gate. Go through and follow waymarks around to the left (by the Ty Canol information board) and through a gap in a wall. At the T-junction, turn left. Keep ahead, now with a fence to your left, and continue to a waymark that directs you sharp right. Climb up out of the wood and keep straight ahead to a gate in the wall ahead, close to the corner of the wood **D**.

Go through and keep ahead with the wall to the right, now with great views all around. Continue past the various cairns that dot the top of the hill, and then continue around left to a double gate, which leads onto a track **E**. Turn left onto the track and follow it downhill to join the road by a cattle-grid. Keep ahead along this road for just over ¼ mile to the burial chamber of Pentre Ifan, reached by turning left through a wooden gate **F** and walking about 200 yds along a path.

Pentre Ifan dates from the Neolithic period, possibly around 3500 BC, and was a chambered tomb for communal burial. What remains is the front of the chamber; the stones that lay to the rear have been removed. This impressive monument lies in a beautiful setting below the slopes of Carningli, overlooking the coast and Dinas Head.

Head back to the road and continue around a left bend and then, as it bends right, turn left through the second gate onto a waymarked footpath. Keep ahead with the hedge to the left and go through a gate, cross a track and go through the right of two gates opposite **G**. Now keep left to a double stile straight ahead. Cross these and keep straight ahead to a gap in the tree-line. Now bear half left to a gate, which leads back into woodland. Follow the path straight through the wood to a gate leading out into a field, and turn left to walk along the left edge of the field to another gate. Keep ahead again, through a narrow scrubby field, and this leads out onto the drive of Pentre Ifan Farm. Turn right to finish.

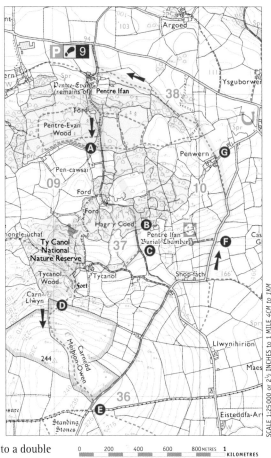

SCALE 1:25 000 or 2½ INCHES to 1 MILE 4CM to 1KM

0	200	400	600	800 METRES	1
					KILOMETRES
					MILES
0	200	400	600 YARDS	½	

Brechfa Forest

		GPS waypoints
Start	Brechfa village car park	
Distance	4 miles (6.4km)	◪ SN 524 302
Height gain	820 feet (250m)	Ⓐ SN 531 304
Approximate time	2½ hours	Ⓑ SN 534 297
Parking	Brechfa village car park	Ⓒ SN 535 285
Route terrain	A real mix of good tracks, muddy paths and quiet lanes	Ⓓ SN 532 282
Dog friendly	Some awkward stiles	
Ordnance Survey maps	Landranger 146 (Lampeter and Llandovery), Explorer 186 (Llandeilo & Brechfa Forest)	

Brechfa Forest has had a chequered past. In the Middle Ages it was a royal hunting ground but by the 19th century, it took on a less glamorous role supplying timber to the industrial valleys of South Wales. It was placed under the care of the Forestry Commission in 1919 and is now managed for timber, recreation and conservation. The beautiful Afon Cothi runs through the forest providing a sylvan focus for this walk.

◪ With St. Teilo's Church to your right and the **Ty Mawr Hotel** to your left, follow the road over the bridge and out of the village to a stile on the right Ⓐ. Cross this and bear slightly left to cross a field to another stile. Cross this and keep straight ahead, along a board walk that crosses a boggy area and leads to another stile by a stream. Cross this stile and a small tributary stream and walk up to a marker post, where you turn right to cross a footbridge. Continue along the obvious track on the other side and then bear around to the right at the top of the hill. Stay with the main track as it bends around to the left and then go through a gate on the right that leads into a wood. Turn immediately left to walk along the bottom of the wood and drop easily to the banks of the Afon Cothi Ⓑ.

This stunning river is the largest tributary of the Afon Tywi and rises up on the Cwmdeudwr Hills north of Llandovery. It eventually empties into the Afon Tywi, near the county town of Carmarthen. It was mined for gold in Roman times and the remains of the mines, which are close to the village of Pumsaint, are now owned by the National Trust and open to the public. The next stretch of the walk is one of the true highlights, following the river downstream past some lovely pools. Keep your eyes open for dippers, grey wagtails and even kingfishers.

Stay with the main path which in places is clear and easy to follow and in others, boggy and rough until it sadly ends at a gate that leads onto a lane by Daren-fawr Farm Ⓒ. Turn right onto the road and climb for a short distance to a drive on the right that leads to Tŷ-llŵyd Farm. Walk up to the farm and keep the house to your right to follow a path that runs alongside it up to a gate **D**. Go through this and join a hedged track which you now follow around to the right and steeply up hill.

Now stay with this clear track as it climbs relentlessly up out of the valley, eventually levelling at the highest point of the walk. Stay with the track as it bends to the right and leads out onto a narrow lane. Turn right onto this and descend steeply down towards Brechfa village. You'll eventually reach a ford, which is usually a little too deep to wade through without getting wet feet. Turn left here and follow this lane up to the main road, where you turn right to return to the village centre and to the car park. ●

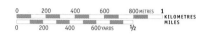

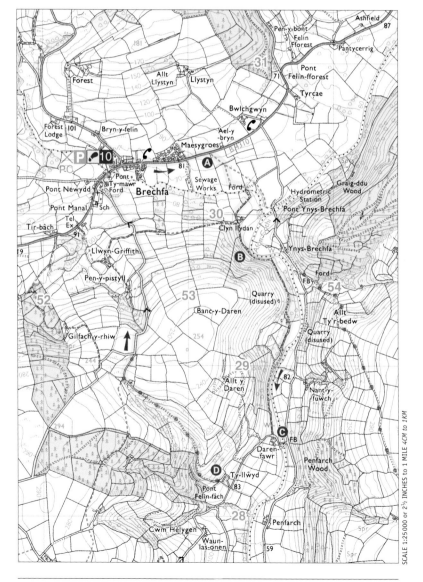

SCALE 1:25 000 or 2½ INCHES to 1 MILE 4CM to 1KM

Blacktar Point, Llangwm and Benton Wood *(vertical side text)*

Blacktar Point, Llangwm and Benton Wood

		GPS waypoints	
Start	Blacktar Point. Take lane signposted to Blacktar Point on northern edge of Llangwm village		SM 998 095
		A	SM 995 094
Distance	4½ miles (7.2km)	**B**	SM 990 092
		C	SM 996 086
Height gain	560 feet (170m)	**D**	SM 994 078
Approximate time	2½ hours	**E**	SM 983 080
Parking	Blacktar Point	**F**	SM 986 092
Route terrain	Shoreline paths, woodland paths, field paths and farm tracks. Some short road sections on a quiet lane		
Ordnance Survey maps	Landranger 158 (Tenby & Pembroke), Explorer OL36 (South Pembrokeshire)		

The mudflats and tree-fringed shorelines of the Daugleddau, the upper reaches of Milford Haven formed by the estuaries of the Eastern and Western Cleddau, Cresswell and Carew rivers, make a scenic contrast with the rest of Pembrokeshire. This easy walk along part of the foreshore and through attractive Benton Wood has fine views across the estuary to the well-wooded shores on the opposite side.

From the car park walk down to the shore and turn right, at a public footpath sign, along a track, which immediately gives fine views across the wide waters of the Daugleddau to the thickly wooded slopes that clothe both shores. The track bears right around Blacktar Point to keep beside Llangwm Pill, one of the many small inlets of the Daugleddau; it bends right again to follow a creek and then turns left across the head of the creek. Here turn left **A** along a tarmac lane towards Llangwm and, when you get to the very head of the inlet, you'll see some stepping stones on the left, crossing the stream. Descend and use them, then turn left on the other side and in a few yards turn

right, at a public footpath sign, up to a lane **B**.

Turn left along the lane and after ¼ mile turn right over a yellow waymarked stile and walk along the right-hand edge of a field, by a hedge on the right. Climb a stile, keep straight ahead to climb another one on the right and then follow the main path leftwards into woodland, dropping to the shore. Turn left along a most attractive path, between woodland on the right and the estuary on the left, and after about 100 yds a yellow waymark directs you to the right **C** up some steps to climb a stile. Now follow a well-waymarked path – yellow signs are painted on tree trunks – through Benton Wood, climbing

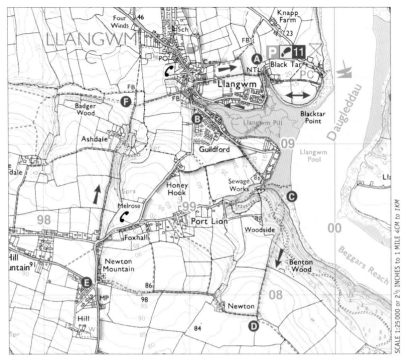

steadily, crossing a track and later continuing along the right-hand edge of the wood. Climb a stile, keep ahead to emerge from the wood and continue along the right-hand edge of a meadow, walking between a line of trees and with a wire fence on the right. After climbing the next stile you join a track **D**.

Boat traffic on the Daugleddau

Turn right onto this and follow it to a farm. The track curves first to the right and then to the left to pass between farm buildings and continues some distance to eventually join a road in the village of Newton Mountain **E**.

Turn right along the road for ¼ mile

Looking across the Daugleddau from Blacktar Point

and at a T-junction cross over and keep ahead along a straight, concrete farm drive. Where the drive bends to the left in front of the gate to Ashdale House, bear slightly right to go through a gate and walk along a lovely woodland path that descends gently to another gate.

Go through, continue through a shallow wooded valley, to another gate and keep ahead along the right-hand edge of a meadow, by a line of trees on the right. About 100 yds before reaching a stile and footbridge at the end of this meadow, turn right **G** through one of the numerous gaps in the line of trees and head straight across a field to climb a double gate, made necessary by the width of the wall.

Cross a brook by a large stone slab and continue along the left-hand edge of a field to another gate. Go through and walk along a track that drops to a stream. Cross it by the bridge and then turn right and right again to cross back to the other side. Now follow the boardwalk and then a narrow path to the road.

Turn left uphill into Llangwm, passing to the right of a church and into the village square. To get to the **Cottage Inn** keep ahead, but the route continues by turning sharp right past a barrier and then right again at the top to curve leftwards into Pill Park Way. Continue along the lane, pass to the right of a cemetery and then, keep left to go through a gate into the sports ground. Keep to the right of the field, passing in front of the grandstand and continuing to the far end, where a gate leads into a field. Continue half right towards the trees ahead, and then drop down a steep path that leads into the wood, going through a gate and descending to the lane at the head of Llangwm Pill **A**, where the outward route is rejoined.

Keep ahead across the head of the small creek and turn right to retrace your steps along the shoreline track to the car park at Blacktar Point. ●

Saundersfoot and Tenby

		GPS waypoints
Start	Saundersfoot	
Finish	Tenby	✎ SN 136 048
Distance	4 miles (6.5km)	Ⓐ SN 138 143
		Ⓑ SN 144 032
Height gain	1,085 feet (330m)	Ⓒ SN 133 021
Approximate time	2½ hours	Ⓓ SN 133 006
Parking	Saundersfoot and Tenby	
Route terrain	Coast path, field edge footpaths and quiet roads	
Ordnance Survey maps	Landranger 158 (Tenby & Pembroke), Explorer OL36 (South Pembrokeshire)	

This walk links the two most popular resorts on the south Pembrokeshire coast. It starts in Saundersfoot and follows a sheltered, highly scenic and unusually well wooded stretch of the coast path, which in the later stages gives super views across to Tenby, an attractive, interesting town well worth exploring at the end. The walk as described is a linear one but there are regular buses between Tenby and Saundersfoot on weekdays and Saturdays, and the train can be used on Sundays.

Tenby combines all the usual amenities of a popular seaside resort with a picturesque aspect and outstanding historic appeal dating back to the Norman Conquest. The old part of the town, its narrow streets confined within medieval walls, occupies a prominent headland. On the north side of the headland attractive, colour-washed, regency and Victorian houses overlook the harbour and a glorious curving sandy beach. On the south side stretches an even more extensive beach. The impressive town walls and the scanty remains of the castle at the tip of the headland, both built in the late 13th century to protect the harbour from Welsh raids, are evidence of Tenby's importance in the Middle Ages as a busy port and staging-post between Bristol and Ireland.

The church also dates from the 13th century but was considerably enlarged during the 15th. The largest parish church in Wales, it reflects Tenby's prosperity at that time, as does the nearby fine Tudor merchant's house. Nowadays the town gets its prosperity mainly from tourism and during the summer months it is thronged with visitors. It has a wide range of hotels, guesthouses, pubs, tearooms and restaurants. Saundersfoot is a lot smaller than Tenby but it still has plenty to offer including a picturesque harbour, which was built originally to export coal, and a lovely main beach.

✎ The walk starts from the seafront in Saundersfoot. Begin by walking down to the quay, with the main beach to the left. If the tide's not high, then turn right to follow the narrow road

Tenby, from the coast path

that runs along the coast, behind the harbour and past the sailing club to the far end of the quay, where a zigzag path leads down to the beach. Follow the beach past one jutting cliff and then look for a set of steps at the far end of the next beach. These lead up to a large fingerpost at the end of a road Ⓐ.

If the tide is too high for this, walk back from the quay to the main road and turn left to take this away from the seafront, swinging around to the left and climbing steeply. Continue to a turning on the left (The Glen), where a Coast Path waymark directs you down the road to the bottom where you meet the path coming from the beach Ⓐ.

Now climb up into woodland for a short distance before dropping steeply into a wooded dell above a stony beach. Climb away from this and go through a gate to follow a field edge for a few paces before another gate leads back into woodland. At a junction of paths, keep left to leave the official Coast Path and drop towards Monkstone Point, with great views. The path eventually turns sharp right, now with views down over Monkstone Beach, and climbs to a waymark at a crossroads of paths, where it rejoins the official Coast Path Ⓑ. To visit the lovely Monkstone Beach, turn left down steps, otherwise,

take the waymarked Coast Path and continue along a lovely stretch of path with views ahead to Tenby.

Continue through a gate and along a field edge then back into woodland, and then along another field edge before dropping steeply to cross a brook in the bottom of Lodge Valley. Climb steeply up again and cross a stile to walk along another field edge before another stile leads into woodland again, where the path leads away from the sea before dropping to cross a footbridge and continuing to a drive above Waterwynch Bay Ⓒ.

Keep ahead to cross the drive, and turn left to follow the path to the left of a gate. At a junction of paths, turn right to climb out of the valley and continue now on an enclosed path that soon starts to drop towards Tenby. Continue down steps to the road and keep ahead until you reach North Beach. Where you can continue along the road or drop down steps to continue along the beach towards the town centre, castle and the picturesque harbour.

To get to the main bus terminal in Upper Park Road, locate the mini-roundabout that separates the High Street, White Lion Street and Norton Street, directly above North beach Ⓓ, and turn down White Lion Road, away from the seafront. Turn left to follow the old walls along South Parade, and then when you reach the war memorial on your right, turn right and right again into Upper Park Road. The bus terminal is a short distance along on the left. ●

0	200	400	600	800 METRES	**1**
					KILOMETRES
					MILES
0	200	400	600 YARDS	½	

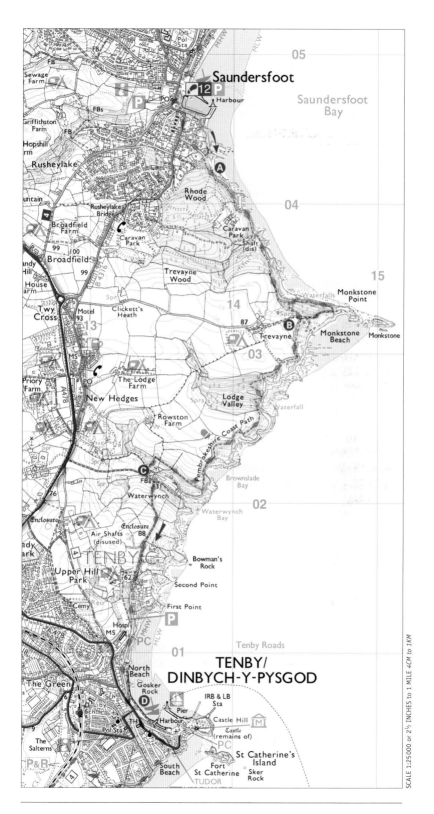

SCALE 1:25000 or 2½ INCHES to 1 MILE 4CM to 1KM

St David's Head and Carn Llidi

		GPS waypoints
Start	Whitesands Bay, north-west of St David's	🖋 SM 734 271
Distance	4½ miles (7.2km). Shorter version 4 miles (6.4km)	Ⓐ SM 723 279 Ⓑ SM 737 287
Height gain	935 feet (285m). Shorter version 625 feet (190m)	Ⓒ SM 736 276 Ⓓ SM 736 272
Approximate time	2½ hours. Shorter version 2 hours	
Parking	Pay and Display car park at the end of the B4583	
Route terrain	Clear coast path and good paths over heathland. Some rocky going on the climb up to Carn Llidi on the longer version	
Dog friendly	No dogs on the Whitesands beach May–September	
Ordnance Survey maps	Landranger 157 (St David's & Haverfordwest), Explorer OL35 (North Pembrokeshire)	

Starting from the glorious sandy sweep of Whitesands Bay, the walk goes around the rocky and rugged headland between the sea and the slopes of Carn Llidi, then turns inland over the shoulder and around the base of Carn Llidi, with a detour to the summit for the magnificent view. Although the coastal part of the walk is rockier than most, there are no particularly strenuous sections. The shorter version omits the summit of Carn Llidi.

Whitesands Bay (Porth Mawr), a curving, mile-long expanse of flat sands, is one of the finest beaches in the country.

🖋 Begin by facing the beach and turn right through a kissing-gate onto the coast path, immediately passing to the right of the site of St Patrick's Chapel, of which there are no visible remains but was supposedly built on the spot where St Patrick originally embarked for Ireland. Keep ahead along the right-hand path at a fork, heading steadily uphill, and follow the path as it curves left to continue above Porthmelgan along to the end of St David's Head Ⓐ. From this wild and often windswept

peninsula the all round views are superb: to the left across Whitesands Bay to Ramsey Sound and Ramsey Island, ahead along the lovely bays of Porth Lleuog and Porthmelgan towards the end of the promontory, and to the right to the distinctive rocky profile of Carn Llidi. At the end of the headland the path turns right to continue in a north-easterly direction, and about 50 yds to the right of it is the burial chamber of Coetan Arthur; it is difficult to spot amid the rocky terrain but lies immediately below the wall of crags ahead. Continue along this wild stretch of coast, between rocks and heather,

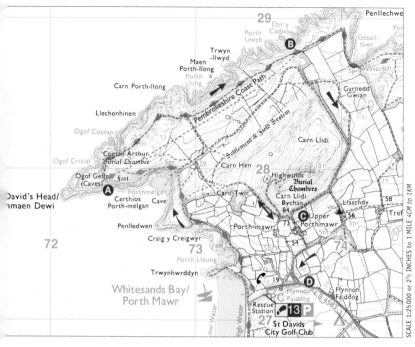

SCALE 1:25 000 or 2½ INCHES to 1 MILE 4CM to 1KM

```
0     200   400   600   800 METRES  1
                                      KILOMETRES
                                      MILES
0     200   400   600 YARDS    ½
```

and on descending into a small hollow be careful not to take the track ahead towards the right shoulder of Carn Llidi but bear slightly left to keep along the coast path. Soon views open up along the north coast of Pembrokeshire.

As you descend into another hollow, look out for a rectangular walled enclosure on the right and a tall fingerpost (you've missed the turning if you reach a hand gate). Turn right off the coast path **B** along a grassy track that heads up to the enclosure and continue, passing to the right of it and heading uphill to a gate-gap.

Go through, climb over the shoulder of Carn Llidi, joining and keeping by a wall on the left, and gently descend along a path that curves to the right around the base of the hill. From this path are extensive views to the left across flat country to St David's Cathedral and the coast of St Bride's Bay beyond.

The path descends to a stile; do not climb it but turn right to continue below Carn Llidi, keeping by a wall on

the left. With more grand views ahead of Whitesands Bay, Ramsey Sound and Ramsey Island, continue to a track **C**.

*Those wishing to omit the detour to the summit should turn left along the track, following the route after **C** below.* Turn right for the ascent of Carn Llidi, taking the right-hand, upper track at a fork and continuing along a rough but well-defined path to the summit. From here the views are magnificent, taking in a great sweep of the Pembrokeshire coast and south-west Wales and on a clear day extending even to the Wicklow hills in Ireland.

Retrace your steps to **C** and continue along the track. Climb a stile beside a metal gate, head down between the farm buildings and continue down a curving, hedge-lined track, later tarmacked, to reach a road **D**. Turn right for the short distance back to Whitesands Bay. ●

Goodwick and Carregwastad Point

		GPS waypoints
Start	Goodwick (Harbour Village). From the centre of Goodwick follow New Hill and continue to where the road ends above Fishguard harbour	☑ SM 949 390
		Ⓐ SM 925 400
		Ⓑ SM 926 404
Distance	5 miles (8km)	Ⓒ SM 932 395
Height gain	755 feet (230m)	Ⓓ SM 936 391
Approximate time	2½ hours	Ⓔ SM 947 388
Parking	Car park in Harbour Village	
Route terrain	Clear coast path and paths and tracks across farmland	
Ordnance Survey maps	Landranger 157 (St David's & Haverfordwest), Explorer OL35 (North Pembrokeshire)	

The route follows a stretch of the Pembrokeshire Coast Path, from above Fishguard harbour to the remote Carregwastad Point, before returning inland by way of the hamlet of Llanwnda. Spectacular views along the rugged coastline are complemented by fine views across grassy moorland to the rocky outcrop of Garnwnda and beyond to the Preseli Hills. There are steep sections along the coast but inland the walking is relatively flat and easy.

Until the beginning of this century Goodwick was a small, obscure fishing village, but after the completion of a rail link in 1906 it aspired to become a major transatlantic port so a large new harbour was constructed. Goodwick enjoyed a brief heyday just before the First World War when it was used by many of the great passenger liners, but its comparative isolation, coupled with the increased size of ships, prevented its development into another Liverpool so it had to be content with a more modest role as a ferry terminal for Ireland.

🐾 From the car park above Fishguard harbour head along the coast path, with impressive views to the right across Fishguard Bay to Dinas Head.

Follow the coast path for about 3 miles to Carregwastad Point, initially a fairly easy walk across a grassy headland but later becoming more rugged and strenuous with several steep ascents and descents. The views are superb: westwards along the coast towards Strumble Head, eastwards towards Dinas Head and Cemaes Head, and inland across to the Preselis.

Soon after following the curve of the large and rugged inlet of Aber Felin you reach a footpath sign Ⓐ. The route turns left here but to visit Carregwastad Point keep ahead, in the direction of a coast path sign, to descend into a steepsided, narrow, wooded valley. Cross a stream and head up the other side, continuing to follow coast path signs to the monument on Carregwastad Point, a magnificent viewpoint **B**. This monument commemorates the landing here by French troops in 1797, the last invasion of Britain. After two days of looting and drunkenness the troops were captured by the local yeomanry and forced to surrender. A more colourful version of this event is that the French decided to lay down their arms after mistaking a crowd of women in their traditional Welsh costume of red cloaks and tall hats for a company of soldiers.

From the monument retrace your steps down and up the steep, wooded valley to the footpath sign at the top of it **A** and turn right to head across a field, at first keeping by a line of gorse bushes on the right and later by a hedgebank and wire fence on the left. Go through a waymarked metal gate in the top corner and follow a path straight across the field ahead; in front is the rocky outcrop of Garnwnda with the village of Llanwnda immediately below it. Go through a second metal gate, walk along a hedge-lined, grassy track to go through a third and continue along the left-hand edge of a field, with a hedgebank on the left, following the field edge as it curves right to a fourth gate. Turn left through this gate and walk along a track that first turns left towards the church and then turns right to go between farm buildings to emerge onto a lane in the scattered hamlet of Llanwnda **C**. This comprises little more than a few houses and a plain church.

Turn left along the lane, passing below Garnwnda on the right. Energetic walkers might like to make a short diversion to climb to the top of it (521 feet/159m) to see the Neolithic burial chamber and enjoy the view. At a T-junction **D** keep ahead along a

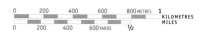

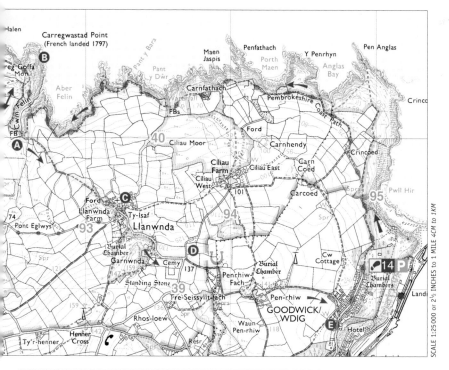

hedge-lined track, continue along the main, left-hand track at a fork and follow it first around a right-hand bend, passing to the left of a house and then around a left-hand bend.

At a farm bear left to pass through a metal gate, go through the farmyard, passing to the right of the house, and continue along a hedge-lined track from which there are more fine views over Fishguard Bay and the Gwaun Estuary. At a fork take the right-hand track, which curves to the right and heads down into Goodwick. On reaching a road **E**, turn left and follow it gently uphill for ¼ mile back to the start. ●

Obelisk on Carregwastad Point

Solva and Pointz Castle

		GPS waypoints	
Start	Solva		
Distance	5 miles (8km)	✍	SM 805 243
Height gain	855 feet (260m)	Ⓐ	SM 803 238
Approximate time	3 hours	Ⓑ	SM 812 240
Parking	National park car park at Solva	Ⓒ	SM 830 237
Route terrain	Farm tracks, field paths and coast path	Ⓓ	SM 827 231
Ordnance Survey maps	Landranger 157 (St David's & Haverfordwest), Explorer OL35 (North Pembrokeshire)		

The route climbs to Cribyn ridge above Solva harbour, a grand viewpoint, descends from it and then heads inland, by way of field tracks and paths, to Pointz Castle. After turning back towards the sea, the return is a splendid cliff-top ramble, later climbing to Cribyn ridge again and descending back into Solva. The walk is outstandingly attractive and yet fairly undemanding.

Solva lies at the head of a narrow, fjordlike inlet, its houses climbing the steep hillsides above the small harbour. This picturesque village and jewel of the Pembrokeshire Coast, was once a port but is now mainly a centre for pleasure craft. Some old limekilns remain on the eastern side of the harbour.

✍ Cross a footbridge in the corner of the car park by the **Harbour Inn**, turn left for a few yards to a footpath sign and turn right to join the coast path. Walk along this tree-lined path that climbs above the harbour, go through a gate-gap and continue steadily up to Cribyn ridge. Continue along the ridge, enjoying the fine views: ahead across St Bride's Bay to Wooltack Point at the end of the Marloes peninsula, and to the right over the narrow, steep-sided inlet, usually full with brightly coloured boats. At the end of this narrow ridge turn left and descend steeply, via steps, into a valley and to a gate.

Go through, cross a footbridge onto a stony beach and walk across it to the base of the cliffs Ⓐ. Turn left along a track, here leaving the coast path, and at a fork take the right-hand track that climbs steadily above the valley; continue along its top edge and go through a gate. About 100 yds farther on, turn left through a gate in a field corner and continue along the track, which bears right to another gate. Go through and keep ahead to pass the remains of St Elvis Cromlech, a Neolithic burial chamber built around 5,000 years ago. Originally, the stones would have been covered by a mound of earth. St Elvis lived in the 6th century and was St David's religious teacher.

Beyond the cromlech, go through a gate, at a public footpath sign, and turn left along an enclosed path parallel to the drive to St Elvis Farm. Go through two gates in quick succession and turn right onto the second broad track, which is actually the farm drive **B**. Where the track bends left, pass through a gate, walk along a straight grassy track, between a hedgebank on the left and a wire fence on the right, and continue along the left-hand edge of a field to go through two successive gates. Keep ahead along the left-hand edge of a field, go through a gate and continue along a narrow, enclosed and possibly overgrown path, going through a series of gates. Eventually, go through one last gate and keep ahead to a public footpath sign; here bear right along a track to Lochvane Farm.

Continue between farm buildings and keep along the track for ½ mile, following it around a left curve. Just where the track bears left towards the next group of farm buildings you reach the overgrown remains of this medieval motte-and-bailey castle, thought to be named after Poncius, a Norman knight who was a tenant of the Bishop of St David's.

Here turn right **C** through a small

gate beyond the large gateway and walk along a grassy path, turn right through a kissing-gate and continue along the top right-hand edge of a field, by a hedge-bank on the right, to a gate. Through it turn left along the left-hand edge of a field, heading downhill, and follow the path as it curves right along the lower edge of the field to a public footpath sign; here turn left through a gate. Continue along a narrow, downhill path between bushes to cross a footbridge over a brook, keep ahead and follow the path around a right bend. This grassy path heads gently downhill towards the sea; at a public footpath sign turn right to rejoin the coast path **D**.

Recross the brook, go through the gate and head

Solva from Cribyn ridge

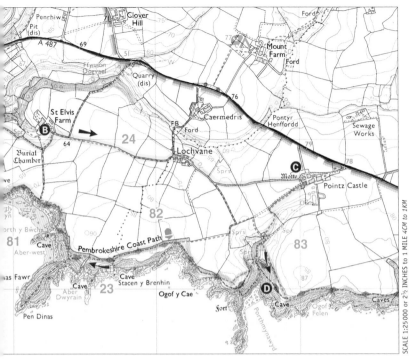

up to the top of the cliffs. Now follow a highly attractive and relatively easy section of the coast path along the cliff tops, enjoying the superb all-round views that take in Newgale Sands, the whole length of the Marloes Peninsula, a glimpse of the oil refineries of Milford Haven, the rugged coastline of the St David's Peninsula looking to Ramsey Island, and views inland of Carn Llidi. In addition you pass above two short rocky peninsulas – Dinas Fach and Dinas Fawr – sandy coves, and then there are fine views of Solva.

Just beyond a coast path sign and above the narrow entrance to Solva harbour, turn sharp right and shortly bear left and descend to the stony beach passed just after the start of the

walk **Ⓐ**. Cross the footbridge and retrace your steps up to Cribyn ridge, turning right at the top. At a fork you can take either the right-hand (upper) or left-hand (lower) path. *Note that if the tide is low, it is possible to walk around the headland on the beach.* ●

_____

Porth Gwyn and Dinas Fawr

Llawhaden and the Eastern Cleddau

		GPS waypoints
Start	Llawhaden	
Distance	5½ miles (8.8km)	🥾 SN 070 173
Height gain	720 feet (220m)	**Ⓐ** SN 068 173
		Ⓑ SN 069 181
Approximate time	3 hours	**Ⓒ** SN 079 181
Parking	At the start	**Ⓓ** SN 083 195
Route terrain	Woodland tracks and paths and	**Ⓔ** SN 091 192
	some paths across farmland	**Ⓕ** SN 075 173
		Ⓖ SN 074 174
Ordnance Survey maps	Landranger 158 (Tenby & Pembroke), Explorer OL36 (South Pembrokeshire)	

Most of this well-waymarked walk is through the attractive woodlands that line both sides of the valley of the Eastern Cleddau upstream from Llawhaden. The last 1½ miles of the route is particularly outstanding, with a delightful mixture of riverside woods and meadows. Llawhaden has considerable historic interest with a fine old church down by the river and the ruins of a medieval castle on the steep wooded bank above.

It is difficult now to envisage the tiny, quiet, off-the-beaten-track village of Llawhaden as an important borough in the Middle Ages, one of the principal possessions of the wealthy and powerful bishops of St David's. Part of its importance came from its situation on the Landsker, the unofficial boundary between the mainly Welsh-speaking area of north Pembrokeshire and English-speaking south Pembrokeshire. Llawhaden Castle was one of several fortresses and palaces that the bishops owned locally and was built to protect their lands from invasions to the north. Its gaunt ruins, principally comprising an imposing 14th-century gatehouse, occupy a ridge above the river. Below the ruins, on the riverbank, is the attractive church, mostly a 14th-century rebuilding of an earlier

structure. Its tall, thin, crenellated tower, which is typical of many in Pembrokeshire, gives the church an almost fortress-like appearance.

🥾 Begin by walking uphill through the village away from the castle. At a bridleway sign turn right **Ⓐ** along a hedge- and tree-lined track that soon gives fine views to the right over the valley of the Eastern Cleddau. The track descends and soon after passing a cottage on the left continues as a narrow path that heads down into a wooded tributary valley.

Ford a small stream, turn right, **Ⓑ** at a footpath sign, along a path that continues through woodland to the left of the stream. The path is likely to be muddy. Go through a metal gate and at a fork a few yards ahead continue along the right-hand path, eventually going through a gate to emerge from the woodland. Cross a minor stream, and turn right along a path, between a wire fence on the left and the stream on the right, to a stile. Climb it, keep ahead and then cross a bridge to continue on the other side for a few paces before crossing back over another bridge and turning right to continue out onto a lane. Turn left, heading uphill and where the lane bears left by a bridleway sign keep ahead along a broad track **C**. The track descends into Drim Wood, passes through a farmyard via a series of metal gates and continues along the righthand edge of steeply sloping woodland. Bear slightly left at a fork to pass through a waymarked gate and continue through the wood. At a

T-junction of tracks cross a small stream and turn right to continue between trees on the left and meadows on the right, climb a stile and keep ahead to a lane in the hamlet of Gelli **D**. A few yards to the left is a typically plain but dignified Welsh 18th-century chapel.

The route continues to the right, crossing the old bridge over the River Syfni just above where it joins the Eastern Cleddau. In front of a railway bridge, turn right in the direction of Narberth and Maenclochog, cross the bridge over the Eastern Cleddau and continue along the lane for another

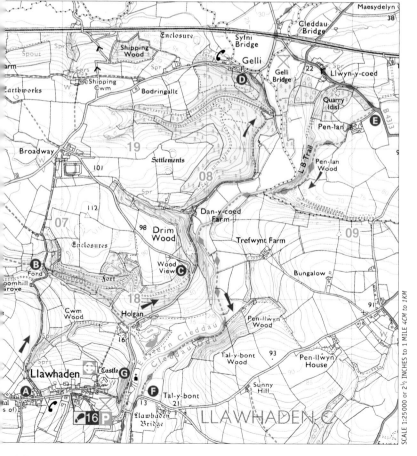

Llawhaden church, on the banks of the Eastern Cleddau

½ mile, heading uphill. At the top, turn right at a footpath sign **E**, go up some steps to climb a stile and walk across a field in the direction of farm buildings. Continue along the left-hand edge of the field to climb a stile – on the skyline ahead the ruins of Llawhaden Castle can be seen – and continue across the next field. Climb another stile, continue along the left edge of a field and at a footpath sign, turn half-right and walk diagonally across the sloping field to climb a stile in the bottom corner. Keep ahead along the right edge of the next field, by woodland on the right, climb another stile and continue steadily downhill, over another stile and down through woodland to join the riverbank.

Now there is a delightful walk back to Llawhaden, mostly by or at one stage above the curving river, partly through the superb oaks of Tal-y-bont Wood and partly across attractive meadows, passing over a series of waymarked stiles and footbridges. Eventually you pass Llawhaden's medieval church on the opposite bank, in a lovely setting immediately below the castle, and climb steps to a lane **F**. Turn right, turn right again to cross the river and turn right again along the lane towards the church.

Opposite the church, turn sharp left at a footpath sign **G** and take the steep, wooded and winding path, passing the castle gatehouse at the top on the return to the village. ●

Cilgerran and the Teifi gorge

			GPS waypoints
Start	Cilgerran Coracle Centre. Follow signs to 'River' from the main street in Cilgerran		✎ SN 197 429 Ⓐ SN 194 430
Distance	6 miles (9.7km)		Ⓑ SN 190 429
Height gain	870 feet (265m)		Ⓒ SN 190 422 Ⓓ SN 195 407
Approximate time	3 hours		Ⓔ SN 205 422
Parking	Coracle Centre car park at Cilgerran		Ⓕ SN 202 427
Route terrain	Field paths, farm tracks, forest paths and quiet lanes		
Ordnance Survey maps	Landranger 145 (Cardigan & Mynydd Preseli), Explorer OL35 (North Pembrokeshire)		

From the banks of the River Teifi the walk begins by heading up into Cilgerran, passing the castle and church, and it continues across fields and through woodland, with attractive views over quiet countryside. It is a twisting route and some muddy sections can be expected but it is well waymarked throughout; simply keep an eye out for the regular yellow arrows. The highlight comes at the end: a glorious stroll through the Teifi gorge with the romantic scene ahead of the towers of Cilgerran Castle rising above the wooded cliffs.

Cilgerran occupies the ridge above the western side of the Teifi gorge, making it an ideal defensive site. The castle, which dates mainly from the early 13th century, and the church, which apart

The towers of Cilgerran Castle above the thickly wooded Teifi gorge

from its fine 14th-century tower is mostly a 19th-century rebuilding, are both in picturesque settings. The Teifi is one of the few rivers in Britain where fishing from traditional coracles can still be seen. It is difficult to believe that this tranquil backwater was once a busy commercial waterway, carrying salmon and later slates downstream to Cardigan. The modern Coracle Centre, where the walk begins, traces the varied history of Cilgerran and its river through the ages.

✎ Facing the river, turn left along a track through the gorge and after a few yards turn left at a footpath sign, following directions to 'Castle and village', up a series of steps. These lead through the remains of former slate quarries, now almost hidden by trees and scrub. In the 19th century Cilgerran became an important slate-quarrying centre with about 300 men employed in the slate industry.

Keep following the signs to 'Castle and village', heading up to pass beneath the castle walls, turning left at the top of steps and turning right along a track in front of a house. By the castle entrance, turn left along a tarmac track towards the village; the main part of the village is to the left but the route turns right here along a lane **Ⓐ**. The lane soon curves to the left and continues towards the church, heading downhill to pass to the right of it. Continue to a bridge over a small stream and turn left just ahead of it onto an uphill wooded path that leads to a road. Turn left and after about 100 yds turn right **Ⓑ**, at a public footpath sign, along a winding, hedge-lined track from which there are pleasant views across fields to hills dotted with woodland.

About 100 yds before reaching a farm, turn right over a stile and then left to head downhill across a field, passing below and to the right of the farm buildings. Continue through a gate and a hedge gap, keep ahead and turn left through a metal gate, immediately turning right **Ⓒ** along an enclosed path. Go through a gate, ford a small stream and turn left alongside it. Keep ahead, passing through a gap, then a gate, then another gap and then another gate by a boggy pond. The path has been diverted at this point and is well-waymarked. First keep the pond to your right and then bear right to cross behind to meet a hedge. Keep this to your right for a few paces to a marker post that directs you left, with a fence to your left. In the corner, turn right, still with the fence to your left and continue to another gate. Go though and continue

in the same direction to a series of marker posts that direct you left and then right and then left again up a steep bank to meet a broad track. Turn left onto this and follow it easily to a cross roads, where you turn left to continue along a pleasant, tree-lined track. After about 100 yds, turn right over a stile and walk along the left-hand edge of a field, by a hedge on the left. Climb a stone stile and continue along the edge of the next field, turning left over another stone stile in the field corner. Now keep along the right-hand edge of a field, by a line of trees on the right, enjoying the fine views ahead of the Teifi Valley. After 50 yds, turn right through a gate. Bear left to walk through lovely grounds and follow the well-waymarked path around to the right, still in the grounds but now with a valley down to your left. Continue as far as you can and then bear left to drop down, over a stile, to a bridge over a stream in the valley floor. Cross this and walk up the other side, with the fence down to your left, until you reach a gate that leads into a field. Turn right and aim to the left of a large barn, where another gate leads onto a track. Turn left onto this and walk along a hedge-lined track to a road **Ⓓ**.

Turn left towards a chapel and almost immediately turn right along a tarmac track signposted to Rhosygilwen. Just after the track curves left, turn right at a public footpath sign and continue along a hedge-lined track, following it gently downhill. At a crossing of tracks climb the stile ahead, continue downhill, turn left at a T-junction and almost immediately turn sharp right onto a woodland path.

For the next 1¾ miles follow the path through attractive mixed woodland, taking care to look out for the indispensable yellow waymarks. In

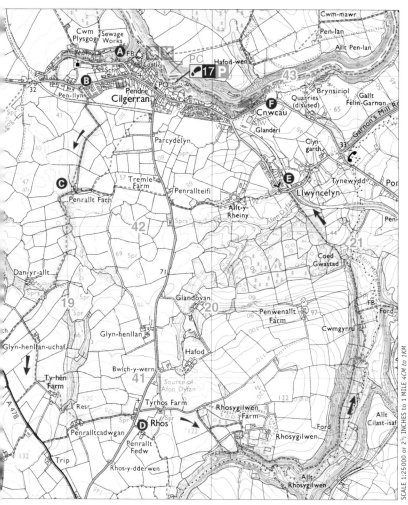

SCALE 1:25000 or 2½ INCHES to 1 MILE 4CM to 1KM

particular watch for a sharp right-hand turn downhill, shortly followed by an equally sharp bend to the left. Another deviation from an otherwise fairly straight route is when you turn left in front of a metal gate and head uphill to turn right over a stile, continuing along the right-hand edge of a sloping meadow and where the wire fence on the right ends, turning right downhill to a track. Turn left along this track and, where it bends right, turn left over a stile, bear right uphill to join a woodland path and turn right along it. Continue through a particularly attractive stretch of lovely broad-leaved woodland, climbing a series of stiles

and crossing several small streams, and finally walk along an enclosed path that heads up to go through a gate and continues to a narrow lane **E**.

Turn left along the lane for ½ mile to a T-junction on the edge of Cilgerran. Turn right along the road and at a public footpath sign turn left **F** onto a path at the side of the **Masons' Arms**. The path soon bends right and heads downhill into the Teifi gorge. Turn left to continue down to the river and follow it back to the start – a superb finale through the thickly wooded gorge. ●

Dale Peninsula

		GPS waypoints
Start	Dale	
Distance	6½ miles (10.4km)	☑ SM 811 058
Height gain	590 feet (180m)	Ⓐ SM 805 057
Approximate time	3 hours	Ⓑ SM 799 058
Parking	Pay and Display car park, Dale	Ⓒ SM 806 028
Route terrain	Coast path and clear paths across farmland	Ⓓ SM 821 052
Ordnance Survey maps	Landranger 157 (St Davids & Haverfordwest), Explorers OL36 (South Pembrokeshire)	

The walk starts by crossing the neck of the Dale Peninsula to the west of Dale village and continues along the coast path around the peninsula to return to Dale. The first part of the walk on the western side is relatively flat and easy; after rounding St Ann's Head walking becomes more energetic along the more hilly and indented eastern shore.

Dale, once an important port and now a popular sailing centre, lies in a valley at the eastern end of the neck of the peninsula. The shallow valley between Dale and Westdale Bay was once covered by the sea, thus making the peninsula an island.

🔖 Begin by walking down to the sea front and turning right, with the sea to your left. Take the first right, before reaching the boatyard, and walk up the street, away from the sea, with houses on either side. Follow this around to the right, and then, as it turns right again, turn left Ⓐ through a gate, at a public footpath sign, and walk along a track that passes to the left of the 19th-century Dale Castle, before turning left. At a public footpath sign keep ahead across grass along a straight and clear path to another gate Ⓑ. Ahead are the impressive cliffs and fine sandy beach of Westdale Bay.

Turn left to join the coast path and follow it initially to the lighthouse on St Ann's Head, the tip of the peninsula. After climbing some steps this is easy, flat walking with impressive scenery, especially approaching St Ann's Head, with a good view to the right of Skokholm Island. Eventually, the coast path swings out onto a lane. Turn right and keep ahead, shortly passing the old lighthouse. Approaching cottages, watch for the coast path leaving on the left. Walk briefly beside a fence and then bear left Ⓒ across the open field towards an old walled garden. Keep going, regaining the clifftops beyond to continue above Mill Bay.

The scenery on this more sheltered side is gentler and more wooded but the coast is more indented, with more ascents and descents. Follow the path around three bays: the first is Mill Bay, where Henry VII landed in 1485 at the start of the campaign that was to lead to his victory over Richard III at Bosworth;

the second is Watwick Bay, at the southern end of which is the West Blockhouse Battery, one of a number of forts built during the mid-19th century to guard Milford Haven at a time of a French invasion scare; and the third is Castlebeach Bay. This part of the walk passes above a number of small, secluded sandy beaches, and there are views to the right across to Milford Haven and the Angle Peninsula.

On the far side of Castlebeach Bay you head towards Dale Point, occupied by another 19th-century fort, now a field studies centre, but before reaching the end of the headland the path turns left across its neck to a stile. Climb it, turn left **D** along a narrow lane above a wooded bank that drops steeply to the sea and follow it for ¾ mile back to Dale.

Laugharne and the Taf Estuary

Start	Laugharne
Distance	6½ miles (10.5km). Shorter version 3 miles (4.8km)
Height gain	770 feet (235m). Shorter version 375 feet (115m)
Approximate time	3 hours (1½ hours for shorter walk)
Parking	Car park next to Laugharne Castle
Route terrain	Clear paths through woodlands and across fields. One steep climb
Dog friendly	Some awkward stiles
Ordnance Survey maps	Landranger 159 (Swansea & Gower), Explorer 177 (Carmarthen & Kidwelly)

GPS waypoints

- SN 301 106
- Ⓐ SN 293 095
- Ⓑ SN 291 098
- Ⓒ SN 299 107
- Ⓓ SN 301 113
- Ⓔ SN 302 119

There is very much a Dylan Thomas theme to this walk. It starts in the small town in which he lived and passes the churchyard in which he is buried and the Boathouse which was his home and workplace for the last four years of his life. There are some moderate climbs, fine wooded stretches and, both at the start and finish, beautiful walking beside the Taf Estuary. The short walk omits the church and Boathouse and final stretch by the estuary.

Although associated with Dylan Thomas almost as much as Stratford-upon-Avon is with Shakespeare, Laugharne, situated on the western side of the Taf Estuary, is a most attractive little town in its own right. Among its attractions is the delightful 18th-century town hall, with a white tower and belfry, and a ruined medieval castle overlooking the estuary. Laugharne Castle dates mainly from the 13th and 14th centuries but in the 16th century it was partly transformed into an Elizabethan mansion by Sir John Perrot.

Dylan Thomas lived in several houses in the town before settling at the Boathouse for the last four years of his life, between 1949 and 1953, with his wife and family. Here, overlooking the 'heron priested' estuary, he wrote some of his finest poetry. The Boathouse, which is passed near the end of the walk, is now a heritage centre dedicated to his life and work.

Begin by facing the estuary and turning right along a tarmac road that becomes a track. Look out for a waymarked post where you bear right across a boardwalk and continue up through woodland above the Taf Estuary to a stile. Climb it, continue below a wooded cliff and at a fork by a Carmarthen Bay Coastal Path information board, take the left-hand downhill path, descending steeply – via steps in places – to a stile. Climb it,

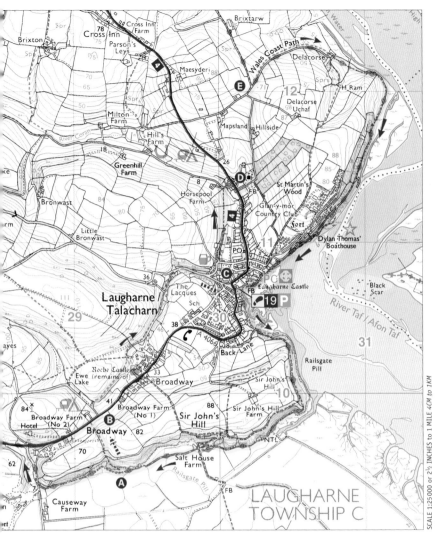

SCALE 1:25 000 or 2½ INCHES to 1 MILE 4CM to 1KM

continue down to climb another one and continue along the edge of marshes and below the wooded cliffs of Sir John's Hill.

Go through a gate, keep ahead but before reaching the next gate in front, turn left through a gate, bear right and continue in the same direction as before, avoiding Salt House Farm. Bear left on rejoining the previous track and about 100 yds after a cattle-grid, look out for a half-hidden, waymarked stile on the right **A**.

Here there is a choice of routes. For

*the easier alternative, continue along the track to a lane in front of a quarry and turn right uphill to the A4066. Turn right to pick up the second alternative at point **B**. For the other alternative – which involves a short but difficult ascent through thick woodland – climb the stile and head steeply up a path, which may be overgrown, to a stile. Climb it, immediately turn right over another one and turn left along the*

Laugharne Castle

left edge of a field. After climbing a stile, head steeply downhill across the next field, climb a stone stile onto the A4066 and turn right **B**. After the rejoining of the two alternative routes, take the first lane on the left, signposted to Llansadurnen. After 50 yds, turn right, at a public footpath sign, along a path through trees to a stile. Climb it, keep ahead by the right edge of a field and where the edge turns right, keep straight ahead to a stile, which you do not cross but instead turn left to walk uphill with the hedge to your right. Follow this around to the right to another stile.

Keep ahead along an enclosed path through woodland, passing to the left of a house, and continue along an enclosed track which eventually curves left to a lane. Turn right to a fork on the edge of Laugharne **C**. *For the shorter walk, take the right-hand lane to return to the start.* If doing the full walk, take the left-hand lane and where it bends sharp right, keep straight ahead along a tarmac track (Holloway Road). At the end of a line of cottages, continue along a path through trees, climb a stone stile, keep ahead across the next two fields and in the corner of the last field, climb a stone stile onto a lane. Turn right to a T-junction, turn right again and just beyond the church lychgate, turn left uphill **D** along a cobbled lane, passing to the right of Laugharne church. Both Dylan Thomas and his wife, Caitlin, are buried here in Saint Martin's churchyard. The graves of Thomas and Caitlin are simply marked by white crosses.

The lane continues uphill between embankments and eventually curves left to a T-junction **E**. Turn right along an enclosed track and at a fork, take the right-hand track which heads downhill into the grounds of a house. Where the track ends, keep right, to cross the grass to a kissing-gate. Now walk along the left-hand edge of a succession of fields to eventually join a path above the tree-lined estuary. Keep ahead through woodland, cross a tarmac track at a bend and continue along an enclosed path, heading gently downhill through woodland. The path becomes a tarmac path beside the estuary and passes above the Dylan Thomas Boathouse. Just beyond the Boathouse, turn left down steps and walk across rocks to join a paved path. Follow it beside the estuary and later below the castle walls to the start. ●

Strumble Head

		GPS waypoints
Start	Garn Fawr. Take unsigned lane ½ mile (800m) north of hamlet of Harmony, which is between St Nicholas and Goodwick (lane leaves road about 200 yds west of Harmony chapel)	✔ SM 898 388 Ⓐ SM 892 388 Ⓑ SM 897 412 Ⓒ SM 913 407 Ⓓ SM 912 396 Ⓔ SM 900 392
Distance	6¾ miles (10.8km)	
Height gain	1,295 feet (395m)	
Approximate time	3½ hours	
Parking	Car park at Garn Fawr	
Route terrain	Clear coast path and paths and tracks across farmland	
Ordnance Survey maps	Landranger 157 (St David's & Haverfordwest), Explorer OL35 (North Pembrokeshire)	

Strumble Head is one of the wildest and loneliest parts of the Pembrokeshire coast. The walk begins just below the prehistoric fort of Garn Fawr on the western side of the headland and follows it round before turning inland and heading across fields and open moorland to return to the start. There is plenty of 'up and down' work but none of the paths is particularly difficult or strenuous, and the glorious coastal views and sense of isolation more than repay the effort spent.

Strumble Head, one of the wildest and most remote stretches of the Pembrokeshire coast

Begin by taking the signposted path at the side of the car park, heading up towards the Iron Age fort of Garn Fawr. *At a waymark either continue ahead over the top of the prehistoric fort of Garn Fawr, enjoying the superb view along the coast from picturesque St David's Head to Cemaes Head, passing the triangulation pillar and descending on the far side, or turn left and follow the grassy path that curves right around the base of the rocky outcrop to join the other path. At the path junction, keep ahead if coming from the top of Garn Fawr or turn left if rounding its base, and head down to farm buildings.* Climb a stile, turn left then turn right onto a tarmac track that leads to the road **A**.

Keep straight ahead to join the coast path and keep along it for nearly 4 miles as it curves around the beautiful, wild, lonely Strumble Head, one of the most rugged sections of the Pembrokeshire coast. There are plenty of ascents and descents and superb views all the way. As you round the head itself, the lighthouse can be seen on an islet; this and several nearby islets create a sort of lagoon.

On reaching a tarmac lane by a car park, turn right along it and where it bends to the right keep ahead through a gate **B** to continue along the coast path. Now you are heading eastwards, and views open up along another rugged stretch of coast looking towards Dinas Head, with Carningli and the Preselis on the horizon. Walk around the large inlet of Porthsychan, ignore the first public footpath sign to the right and continue along the coast path as far as a collection of footpath signs just before reaching a bungalow **C**.

Here bear right through a gate and keep ahead across a field, passing through a gap in the wall and continuing across a boggy area, parallel to a wire

fence on the left, to a stile. Climb it, keep ahead to join a track and bear right along it. Follow this winding track through several gates, later heading steadily uphill to go through a metal gate onto a lane. Turn left along it, then turn right **D** through the first farm gate to walk past the barn and then turn left to walk to the right of the farmhouse.

Go through a metal gate and

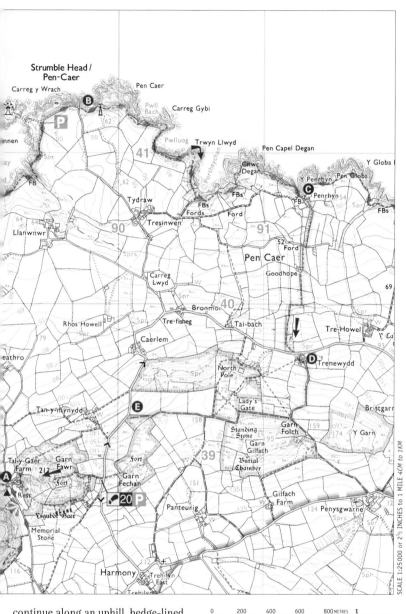

Strumble Head / Pen-Caer

continue along an uphill, hedge-lined track. The track first bends right and later bends left to a metal gate; go through it and keep ahead for a few yards to a T-junction of paths and tracks.

Turn right onto a path that keeps along the bottom edge of open grassy moorland, roughly parallel with a hedge-bank on the right. At first keep in a straight line but later the path bends first to the left and shortly afterwards to the right to continue between hedge-banks, with a striking view of Garn Fawr in front. Finally, head through an area of bracken to a footpath sign and onto a lane **E**. Turn left uphill for just over ¼ mile to return to the starting point. ●

Newcastle Emlyn and Cenarth

		GPS waypoints
Start	Newcastle Emlyn	☑ SN 309 407
Distance	6½ miles (10.5km)	Ⓐ SN 305 403
Height gain	1,015 feet (310m)	Ⓑ SN 300 409
Approximate time	3½ hours	Ⓒ SN 281 410
Parking	Newcastle Emlyn	Ⓓ SN 269 416
Route terrain	Woodland paths, farm tracks and	Ⓔ SN 275 419
	riverside paths. Some road walking	Ⓕ SN 282 416
Dog friendly	Care needed on main roads	Ⓖ SN 293 420
Ordnance Survey maps	Landranger 145 (Cardigan & Mynydd Preseli), Explorer 185 (Newcastle Emlyn)	

This varied and attractive walk is in the Teifi Valley on the Carmarthenshire–Ceredigion border. The first half is mostly along enclosed tracks and paths on the south – Carmarthenshire – side of the river. After passing the spectacular Cenarth falls and walking through a beautiful wooded gorge beside the Teifi, the return leg is along quiet lanes and woodland paths above the river. On the final stretch, there are grand views over the valley to Newcastle Emlyn.

The hilltop town of Newcastle Emlyn occupies a virtual peninsula, almost encircled by the River Teifi. The ruins of the mainly 13th century castle, from which the town gets its name, stand on the narrowest part of the peninsula and mainly comprise a gatehouse and a few walls.

[✎] Start by the old Town Hall, with the castle and Castle Street at your back, and turn left to walk along Sycamore Street. Just after the main road curves left, turn right along Porth Street, a short linking road that leads to the A484, where you turn right. Take the first road on the left, signposted to Capel Iwan and Leisure Centre, and at a public bridleway sign, turn right along a track 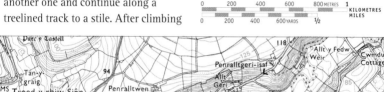 **A**. The track descends through trees and past a house to a footbridge beside a ford. Cross the

Castle ruins at Newcastle Emlyn

bridge and head uphill, bending right and continuing up to a lane.

Turn right downhill and at a public footpath sign, turn left along a tarmac track **B**. Go through a gate by farm buildings, keep ahead to go through another one and continue along a treelined track to a stile. After climbing

it, head downhill, climb another stile and keep ahead to the A484 again **C**. Continue along the enclosed tarmac track opposite and at a footpath post, turn left along a tree-lined path. Go

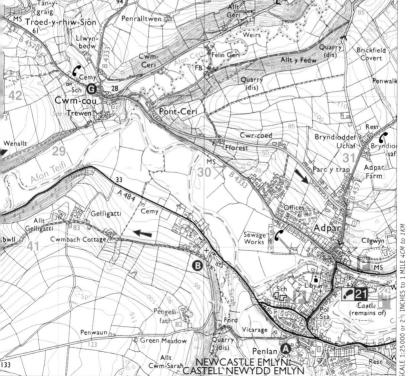

through two gates in quick succession, keep ahead along an enclosed track and where the main track bends right to a house, keep ahead along a grassy track to a gate.

Go through, continue gently downhill along the left edge of a field, go through a gate and walk along an enclosed path. After passing in front of a house, keep straight ahead along an enclosed path to the right of a church and continue down a track beside the **Three Horseshoes pub** to a road. Turn right into Cenarth, cross the bridge over the River Teifi – here entering Ceredigion – and turn right **D** along a path that passes beside a car park and the Cenarth Falls. In full spate, the falls are a most impressive sight. Beside them is the National Coracle Centre in the grounds of a 17th-century flour mill. For centuries Cenarth was a centre of coracle fishing.

Look out for where you climb steps and continue along a path through a wooded gorge above the river, a most attractive part of the walk. The path later bends left away from the river and heads uphill along the right inside edge of sloping woodland to a gate. Go through, turn right **E** along a winding lane, and just after a left bend by a farm, turn right through the kissing-gate **F**. Walk half right across a field, go through another kissing-gate on the far side, turn left and continue along the left inside edge of woodland. Gaps

Cenarth Falls

in the trees reveal fine views over the valley to the right.

The path descends to a stone stile. Climb it, keep ahead along a tree-lined path which emerges onto a lane and the lane curves left to a road in Cwm-cou **G**. Turn sharp right and take the second lane on the left, signposted as a No Through Road. Cross a bridge over a stream and continue along the lane which briefly runs parallel to the main road and then ascends through trees, giving superb views over the valley and Newcastle Emlyn.

At a T-junction in Adpar, turn right and descend steeply, curving left to the bridge over the Teifi. Cross it and head uphill to the start. ●

Treffgarne gorge and mountain

			GPS waypoints
Start	Nant-y-Coy Mill		🔖 SM 956 252
Distance	7 miles (11.3km)		**Ⓐ** SM 958 247
Height gain	835 feet (255m)		**Ⓑ** SM 960 247
Approximate time	3½ hours		**Ⓒ** SM 959 228
Parking	Lay-by at Nant-y-Coy Mill, on the A40, 6 miles north of Haverfordwest		**Ⓓ** SM 959 230
			Ⓔ SM 956 236
			Ⓕ SM 955 244
Route terrain	Mainly rough paths across farmland. Some woodland and some short sections on tarmac. Care needed on the A40		**Ⓖ** SM 953 245
			Ⓗ SM 938 239
			Ⓙ SM 932 250
Dog friendly	Some awkward stiles and care needed on the main road		
Ordnance Survey maps	Landranger 158 (Tenby & Pembroke), Explorer OL35 (North Pembrokeshire)		

An initial walk through the attractive woodlands that clothe the eastern side of the Treffgarne gorge above the Western Cleddau river is followed by a circuit of the bare, grassy moorland of Great Treffgarne Mountain. The combination of wooded gorge and open moorland makes for a walk of great scenic variety, and from the higher points there are extensive views, especially looking towards the Preseli Hills. Great Treffgarne Mountain rises only to the modest height of 531 feet (162m) and, although there are several ascents and descents during the walk, these are lengthy and gradual rather than steep or strenuous. This walk involves crossing some boggy terrain and fording a stream so appropriate footwear should be worn, especially after rain.

The walk starts by Nant-y-Coy Mill and bridge at the entrance to Treffgarne gorge, where the main road, railway and river all squeeze through the narrow gap below Great Treffgarne Rocks on the western side of the gorge and Little Treffgarne Rocks on the eastern side.

🔖 Begin by walking south along the A40 through the gorge; it is a busy road but there is a footpath beside it for most of the way. After passing a sign pointing right, look out for a footpath sign (set back) and turn left **Ⓐ** onto a grassy path, which leads through an area of bracken, gorse and trees, descending by steps to cross first the railway line and then the Western Cleddau to enter woodland. Keep straight ahead to cross a boggy area before heading uphill through trees.

At a waymarked post, turn right **B** to scramble up onto a rather indistinct path that continues through the woodland, above a flat area that was an embankment built by Brunel as part of the route of his railway link to Ireland, aborted in 1851 as a result of the Irish potato famine. Initially the path is not easy to spot or clear to follow but it climbs steadily all the time through mixed woodland towards the ridge. Later it becomes more obvious and curves left to head more steeply up to the top edge of the woodland. Turn right to walk along the top edge of the woodland, by a wire fence on the left; from here there are superb views to the right across the gorge to the prominent rocky outcrops of Maiden Castle and Poll Carn. After a while the path veers away from the top edge and continues through conifers to a stile. Climb the stile and continue along a delightful section of the walk through the broadleaved woodland of Little Treffgarne Wood. At a waymarked post, keep ahead a few yards to go through a gate and join a drive and follow it as it winds downhill, crosses a stream and continues as a tarmac lane, passing

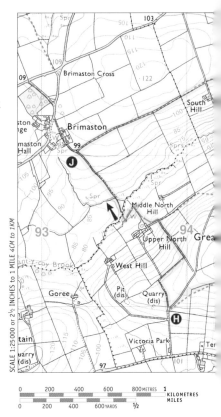

St Michael's Church, Treffgarne

under a railway bridge to reach the main road **C**.

Turn right along the road – there is a footpath – cross the river and take the first turning on the left **D**, signposted to Treffgarne. Follow the winding uphill lane for ½ mile, passing through the village, and where it bends sharply to the left by a small church keep ahead **E** along a pleasant, treelined concrete track to Mount Pleasant Farm. Ahead are the volcanic rocky outcrops of Maiden Castle and Poll Carn. Pass through a gate to the left of

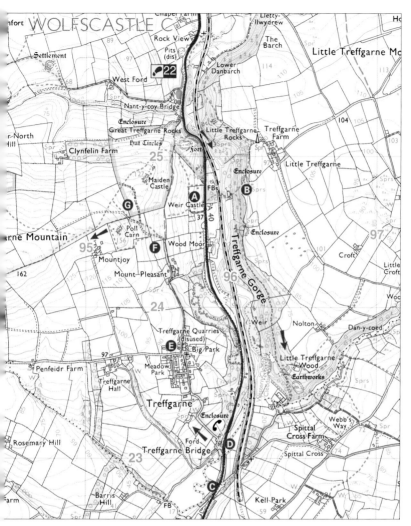

the farm, the track now becoming rough, go through a metal gate and turn left **F** to head towards Poll Carn. Use the track that crosses open grassland, keeping to the left-hand track where the path forks until you arrive at another gate and a yellow-waymarked post **G**. Go through the gate, turn left and with the fence on your left make for a waymarked stile in the top left-hand corner of the field to the right of Poll Carn.

Climb the stile and continue alongside a hedgebank, going over several stiles and climbing gently to the summit of Great Treffgarne Mountain, marked by an overturned triangulation pillar on the other side of the wire fence on the left. Although the summit is rather bare and featureless, the all-round views are superb, southwards towards Milford Haven and northwards to the bold outlines of the Preseli Hills.

Continue by the wire fence on the left, descending almost imperceptibly, and where the fence turns to the left keep ahead to a metal gate and concrete stile. Cross the stile and turn left along the track to a T-junction and here turn right **H** along an uphill tarmac track.

Over the rise, bend right, but at the next bend, go left through a gate and continue at the field edge. Emerging through another gate at the far side, turn downhill along a grass track. At the bottom, cross to the gate opposite and bear left to another gate near the bottom field corner. Follow the path away over a ditch, shortly swinging right through trees to find a clapper bridge over Nant-y-coy Brook. Keep ahead to emerge onto the end of a stone track. Follow it up the hill.

After ¼ mile, turn off right **J** along an attractive, grassy, enclosed track. This is another lovely part of the walk, and over to the right there are fine views across the expanses of Great Treffgarne Mountain, with Maiden Castle and Poll Carn both peeping above the skyline.

Climb a stile to keep ahead along a rougher and more uneven path, climb another stile and continue along the right-hand edge of a field, by a wire fence on the right, to a third stile. Climb that, keep ahead, cross a lane and now continue, by a hedgebank on the right, to climb a stone stile. Continue down the right-hand edge of the field to arrive at a stile constructed of wooden railway sleepers. Cross this and turn immediately right (waymarked) to another stile of sleepers allowing access to a field with a circular enclosure, the site of an ancient settlement. Turn half left to walk diagonally across the field and pass the settlement, continuing downhill to a metal gate in the bottom corner of the field. Go through, walk along a hedge-lined track and where the track bends right, go through another gate, passing to the left and rear of a farmhouse, and along the track, which descends to the A40. Turn right to return to Nant-y-Coy Mill. ●

Maiden Castle on Treffgarne mountain

Wooltack Point and Marloes

		GPS waypoints	
Start	Martin's Haven near Marloes village	🔳	SM 760 089
Distance	7 miles (11.3km)	Ⓐ	SM 754 093
		Ⓑ	SM 760 088
Height gain	425 feet (130m)	Ⓒ	SM 781 076
Approximate time	4 hours	Ⓓ	SM 781 082
		Ⓔ	SM 787 082
Parking	National Trust car park at Martin's Haven (fee)	Ⓕ	SM 786 085
		Ⓖ	SM 785 089
Route terrain	Coast path and clear paths across farmland. Two short sections on narrow lanes		
Ordnance Survey maps	Landranger 157 (St David's & Haverfordwest), Explorer OL36 (South Pembrokeshire)		

Dramatic cliff scenery, sandy beaches, superb views and relatively flat walking make for the perfect coastal walk. The narrow Marloes Peninsula forms the southern arm of St Bride's Bay, with the headland of Wooltack Point at its tip. Apart from crossing the neck of the peninsula near Marloes village, the walk keeps by the sea all the while, following the coast round.

🔳 At the far end of the car park, walk along a lane down to where the lane bears right to the jetty at Martin's Haven by some stone gateposts. The posts are in a wall built to enclose a deer park that it was planned to establish here in the 18th century, but the plan never materialised. Pass between the posts, go through a gate and keep ahead up steps to do a circuit of this proposed deer park, passing a coastguard lookout hut and continuing to Wooltack Point Ⓐ, the rocky headland at the western tip of the Marloes Peninsula. This is a magnificent viewpoint: to the right you look across St Bride's Bay to St David's Head, and to the left and ahead are the offshore islands of Skokholm and Skomer, both important sanctuaries for birds and grey seals.

From Wooltack Point turn sharply left along the cliffs, later following a line of yellow-topped posts to reach a gate Ⓑ just south of the starting point. Go through and turn right to walk along

Marloes Sands

The beautiful beach at Marloes Sands

the rugged south coast of the peninsula, with fine views to the right of Skokholm Island, passing by the rocky, flat-topped Gateholm Island, and later keeping above the fine, flat, long beach of Marloes Sands.

Descend some steps into a narrow, steep-sided valley and at the bottom turn left **C**, leaving the coast path, to head up a well-surfaced track. This bends sharply to the left, later curves right and continues to a lane **D**. Turn right along it for nearly ½ mile and, just after passing a farm on the right, turn left **E** through a gate at a public footpath sign, and walk along the right-hand edge of a field, by a hedgebank and wire fence on the right. Climb a stile and keep ahead, climbing another stile onto a road. To see the village of Marloes with its church and clock tower, and to visit the **Lobster Pot Inn**, turn right, but the route continues to the left along the road as far as a public footpath sign, where you turn right through a gate **F**.

Walk along the right-hand edge of a field towards the sea and at the bottom end follow the direction of a public footpath sign to the left to continue along a narrow path. At a fork take the left-hand path, shortly rejoining the coast path **G** and follow it for the next

two miles, now along the north side of the peninsula but with the same combination of fairly easy walking and spectacular cliff scenery as before. On reaching the cove of Martin's Haven, bear left and descend to a tarmac lane.

Turn left along it to the stone gateposts bordering the 'deer park' and turn left again to return to the car park. ●

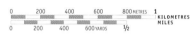

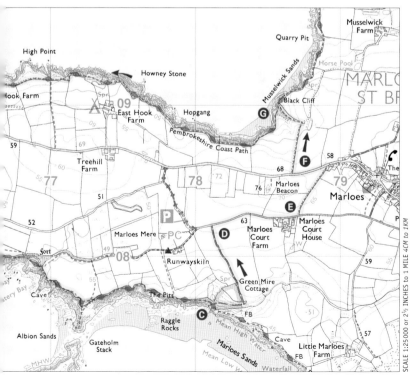

Gwaun Valley and Carningli

Start	Pontfaen
Distance	8 miles (12.9km)
Height gain	1,180 feet (360m)
Approximate time	4 hours
Parking	Pontfaen
Route terrain	Mainly forest tracks, many muddy, then a long climb onto open moorland. Some quiet lanes
Dog friendly	Some awkward stiles
Ordnance Survey maps	Landrangers 145 (Cardigan & Mynydd Preseli) and 157 (St David's & Haverfordwest), Explorer OL35 (North Pembrokeshire)

GPS waypoints	
🖉	SN 024 339
Ⓐ	SN 037 339
Ⓑ	SN 053 345
Ⓒ	SN 057 353
Ⓓ	SN 060 359
Ⓔ	SN 054 366
Ⓕ	SN 038 364
Ⓖ	SN 036 360
Ⓗ	SN 041 351

This lengthy but highly attractive walk through the beautiful, secret Gwaun Valley offers the walker the best of all worlds: an initial ramble through delightful broad-leaved woodlands, followed by a climb to the slopes of the open moorland of Carningli – from where there are extensive views over the valley, Preselis and coast – and finally a descent back into the wooded valley. All the ascents and descents are steady and gradual but some muddy sections are likely on the woodland paths and tracks during the first part of the walk.

🖉 Start by taking the wooded riverside path that leads from the car park; this is a most attractive path below sloping woodland to the right, above the River Gwaun on the left and with lovely views up the valley. After a modest climb, descend to a footbridge Ⓐ, cross it and keep straight ahead to a footpath sign about 50 yds ahead. Here keep ahead again to climb a stile and continue through this delightful woodland.

At a fork, bear right along the upper path, passing above a ruined building, head steadily up to a stile, climb it and continue uphill to reach the top edge of the woods. From this high point there

are superb views over the Gwaun Valley. Continue, climb another stile and keep ahead to a junction in front of Tregynon Farm **B**. Bear left, turn left and then left again to follow a grassy track along the top right-hand edge of woodland, passing an impressive waterfall. The track bears right to a metal gate; go through it and descend along an enclosed, tree-lined, grassy path to a junction on the valley floor. Turn sharp right, in the direction of Gellifawr and Llanerch, and continue to a footbridge. Cross it, bear right by the stream for a few yards and then bear left along a path through the trees. Initially it may be rather boggy but the worst is bridged by a succession of logs that act as stepping stones and soon the path climbs above the valley bottom and conditions underfoot improve.

Turn left at a junction with a fingerpost and continue through more

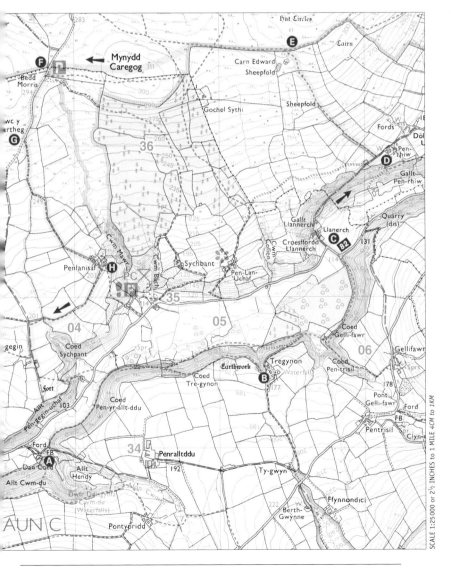

pleasant woodland, eventually passing through a gate onto a lane. Turn left and, where the lane bends sharply to the left, keep ahead **C** through a gate along a concrete drive to Llanerch Farm. Go through another gate just to the left of the farmhouse, continue along an uphill track and after 50 yds fork right to continue along an enclosed, tree-lined track, climbing steadily all the while through woodland and passing through two more gates to reach another junction of tracks near farm buildings **D**.

Here turn left along another enclosed uphill track, going through a succession of gates and stiles and keeping along the right-hand edge of fields, with a hedgebank and wire fence on the right most of the time. Eventually you emerge into a large open field. Keep ahead – there is no visible path – to a gate in the next fence and then continue to the right of two prominent rocky outcrops before bearing slightly left to climb a stile which leads onto open moorland. Turn left **E** alongside a wire fence on the left and over to the right are the remains of a prehistoric fort and hut circles that litter the summit of Carningli.

After nearly ½ mile where the fence turns sharply to the left bear half left to follow a clear path towards the top of Mynydd Caregog. There are now extensive views across the wild, open, heathery moorland, especially over the Gwaun Valley to the line of the Preseli Hills and to the coast. Keep straight ahead and continue in a straight line across the moorland to reach a narrow lane and parking area at Bedd Morris **F**, a Bronze Age stone standing by the roadside.

Turn left along the lane for ¼ mile and at a public footpath sign bear left **G** over a cattle-grid to walk along a broad farm track. Follow the track gently downhill around several bends to a farm, pass to the right of the farm and turn right **H** through the second and lower one of two metal gates on the right. Continue along the right-hand edge of several fields, by a hedgebank on the right all the while, curving gradually to the right and passing through a series of gates and stiles.

At a footpath sign, turn left down a track, go through a metal gate to pass to the right of a farmhouse and ahead are two metal gates. Go through the left-hand waymarked one, continue along an enclosed track, which later opens out, and keep ahead along the right-hand edge of a field to a gate in the bottom corner. Go through the gate and bear right along a flat grassy path that keeps along the top right-hand edge of woodland, by a hedgebank on the right. It descends gently and finally bends sharply to the left and descends more steeply to a metal gate onto a road.

Go through the gate, turn sharp right and follow the road for ¾ mile back to Pontfaen.

Looking across the Gwaun Valley to the Preseli ridge

Angle Point and West Angle Bay

		GPS waypoints
Start	West Angle Bay	
Distance	9 miles (14.5km)	✒ SM 854 031
Height gain	1,195 feet (365m)	Ⓐ SM 841 027
		Ⓑ SM 878 007
Approximate time	4½ hours	Ⓒ SM 875 021
Parking	At start	Ⓓ SM 873 033
Route terrain	Coast path, field edge footpaths and quiet roads	
Ordnance Survey maps	Landranger 157 (St David's & Haverfordwest), Explorer OL36 (South Pembrokeshire)	

Angle Point marks the place where the Pembrokeshire Coast Path National Trail rejoins the cliff tops after its lengthy diversion inland around the headwaters of Milford Haven. It's a scenic watershed with the busy but calm waters of the Haven on one side and the turbulent surf of the Atlantic on the other. This walk traces the coast around the narrow headland, taking in some wonderfully rugged scenery on the way out, and then passing close to one of West Wales' finest beaches, Freshwater West, before returning on the Haven side of the point, following field-edge paths high above the busy waterway. The various watchtowers and battlements point at the obvious military significance of these waters.

The walk could be started from Angle village, which is easier to reach than the beach car park, but there's limited parking on the narrow streets so it's probably best to continue down to West Angle Bay, where there's plenty of space.

✒ Start by continuing down towards the sea and then taking the footpath that leads left beside the **café**. Continue past the public conveniences and go through a gate to cross a field to a gate on the other side. Continue through a succession of gates and you'll eventually emerge up on the cliff tops, close to a sharp headland crowned with

a tower Ⓐ. This can be reached by following the clear path out and back but *care is needed as the ground is very steep.*

Continue along the coast path, passing through further gates and eventually dropping to a footbridge. Cross this and continue past Sheep Island on your right. The next section is quite strenuous as the path dips into and climbs out of a succession of deep valleys, all the time with great views over the wonderful coastline. Continue towards the beautiful beach of Freshwater West and as you approach the sands, look for a footpath waymarker to the left **B**.

Cross the stile and follow the path up the shallow valley and leftwards to a stile at the top. Cross this and keep straight ahead across the next field to yet another stile. Cross this and continue to the B4320. Turn left onto the road and continue past a row of houses before taking a turning on the right. This leads to the shores of the estuary, where you turn left onto the coast path **C**, which immediately merges with a drive. Continue along this to a waymarked bridleway on the right – this is known as the ridge and crosses the estuary at low tide shaving a short distance off the walk. If it does not look amenable, keep ahead to join the road that leads into Angle village. Turn right by the church onto a muddy track and then follow this over a bridge at the

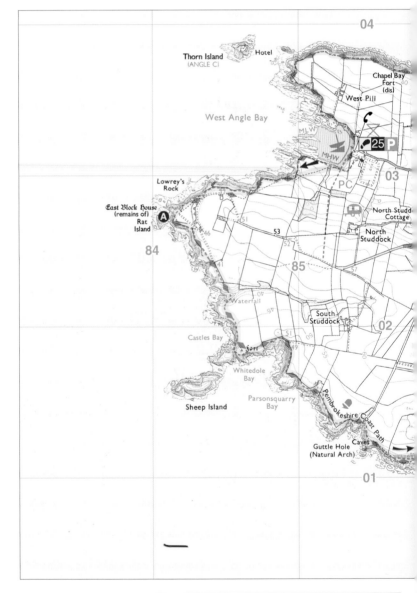

head of the inlet before continuing around to the right.

Continue easily past the **Old Point House Inn**, which you keep on your left, and then follow field edges to a gravel turning bay above the lifeboat station **D**. Keep straight ahead, through a gate, and now continue along the edge of a number of fields and into a wooded area, where you join a track that loops around some holiday cottages to the entrance of Chapel Bay Fort, now open as a military museum with another welcome **café**. Leaving the track, keep ahead past the fort to regain the coast beyond, shortly rounding the point overlooking Thorn Island. The island is topped by a fort that was built to protect the waters of the Haven from a

French invasion. These days it is a hotel.

Stay with the coast path past the island and continue as it descends into West Angle Bay. A brief diversion sidesteps a landslide but other than this, it's easy to follow, eventually merging with a drive that leads back down to the car park.

Sandstone sea cliffs near Angle Point

St David's, Porth Clais and Ramsey Sound

Start	St David's	
Distance	9 miles (14.5km)	
Height gain	770 feet (235m)	
Approximate time	4½ hours	
Parking	Main Pay and Display car park east of St David's	
Route terrain	Clear coast path and tracks across farmland	
Ordnance Survey maps	Landranger 157 (St David's & Haverfordwest), Explorer OL35 (North Pembrokeshire)	

GPS waypoints

- 🖉 SM 757 252
- Ⓐ SM 751 249
- Ⓑ SM 751 243
- Ⓒ SM 740 242
- Ⓓ SM 723 252
- Ⓔ SM 735 254
- Ⓕ SM 737 250
- Ⓖ SM 742 251

There can be few finer coastal walks than this one. From St David's the coast is reached in ½ mile and then the route follows it around from St Non's Bay to Porthstinian, an outstandingly wild, beautiful and lonely stretch of coastline, which is also relatively easy for walking, with a well-defined path and only a few modest ascents and descents. For much of the way the tower of St David's Cathedral and indeed the unrivalled collection of medieval buildings at St David's, together with other sites on the way that are associated with the life of the Welsh patron saint, add considerable historic and architectural appeal to a walk of the highest scenic quality. Plenty of time should be allowed for a thorough exploration of these.

There is a feeling of isolation about St David's, situated on a remote peninsula at the south-western tip of Wales, but in the Dark Ages the holy city of Wales was an important centre of the Celtic world, lying at the crossing of routes linking Wales, Ireland, England, Cornwall and Brittany. It has the distinction of being the smallest city in Britain and, far from being dominated by the cathedral, only the upper part of the tower can be seen from the 14th-century cross in the centre of what is little more than a village. This is because St David's Cathedral, far and

away the most imposing of the Welsh cathedrals, lies in the valley of the little River Alun, built there so as not to be seen from the sea by Viking raiders. It occupies the site of a monastery allegedly founded by St David early in the 6th century and became an important place of pilgrimage, especially after 1120 when the Pope decreed that two visits to the shrine of St David were the equivalent of one to Rome; three equalled a journey to Jerusalem itself.

The cathedral is reached by passing through the medieval Tower Gate

(Porth-y-Tŵr) and descending a flight of steps. This beautiful, austere building, the fourth on the site, is built of the unique, purple-coloured local stone, and its bulk seems to fill the valley. It is basically Norman, built in the late 12th century, but with a Gothic east end, which was the result of a rebuilding necessitated by the collapse of the central tower in 1220. The most outstanding features of the interior are probably the massive rounded pillars of the nave, the ornate 15th-century timber ceiling and, behind the high altar, the casket containing the bones of the patron saint of Wales.

A few yards away, on the other side of the river, is the remarkable Bishop's Palace, built in the 13th and 14th centuries and one of the finest buildings of its kind. Its size and splendour is a reflection of the enormous wealth and power of the medieval bishops of St David's. Particularly impressive is the 14th-century Great Hall with its extraordinary arcaded parapet.

👢 Turn left out of the car park and walk down the road towards the coast. Turn right beyond the houses and then turn left on to a waymarked bridleway. Follow this easily between hedges and past the end of a road. Continue to a junction with a lane **Ⓐ**, where you turn left to continue down towards the sea. After the lane ends, keep straight ahead through a metal kissing-gate and continue along a track. Just before reaching the sea and a large house, turn right **Ⓑ** onto a grassy path that heads down to St Non's Well and a few yards beyond that the meagre ruins of St Non's Chapel. The chapel is traditionally associated with St Non, mother of St David, who is supposed to have given birth to him here during a thunderstorm in about AD 500. The well is alleged to have sprung up at the same time.

From the ruins continue across the field, climb a stone stile and turn right to join the coast path. The route now follows the coast path around the south-west tip of Wales to Porthstinian, a superb walk which passes some outstanding cliff scenery and gives a succession of magnificent views. Among the highlights is the detour around the harbour of Porth Clais **Ⓖ**, about ½ mile after joining the coast

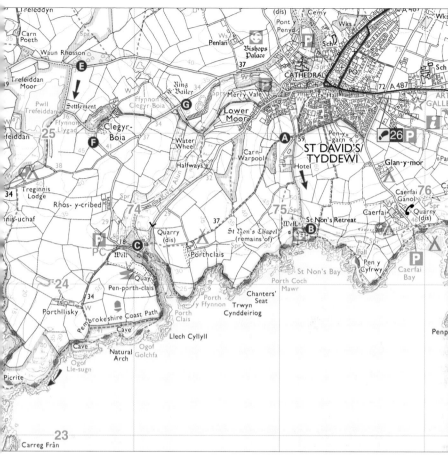

path, where the River Alun flows into the sea. It is hard to believe that this narrow inlet was once an important harbour serving St David's; a few old cottages, the harbour walls and some limekilns are all that survive. The next highlight is the spectacular Porthlysgi Bay, where there is a brief descent to the beach, and as you continue Ramsey Island fills the horizon. After a definite turn to the right, the path continues northwards with fine views across Ramsey Sound to the island, a wildlife sanctuary.

The path eventually meets a lane at St Justinian's **D**, where old and new lifeboat stations stand side by side perched above the rocky bay. Follow the lane uphill, past the 16th-century

ruins of St Justinian's Chapel, built on the site of the Celtic chapel founded by St Justinian, friend and colleague of St David. After passing a parking area, continue ahead along the road and soon the houses and cathedral tower of St David's come into view; to the left the distinctive profile of Carn Llidi above St David's Head can be seen.

After ¾ mile turn along the first lane on the right **E**, which bends sharply to the left, heading towards the prominent rocky outcrop of Clegyr-Boia, then bears right and heads gently uphill. At the top, where the lane bends to the right, bear slightly left **F** along a broad

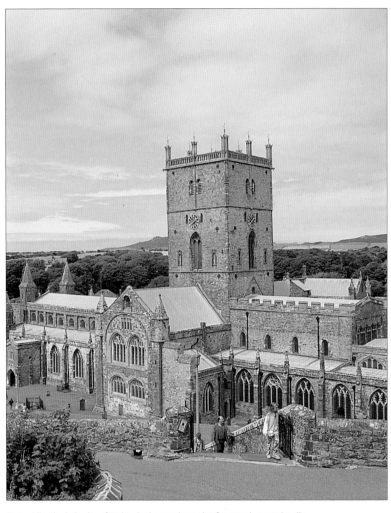

St David's, the holy city of Wales, is the starting point for superb coastal walks

track, passing below Clegyr-Boia and to the left of farm buildings. Clegyr-Boia is an Iron Age hill-fort occupied in the 6th century by an Irish pirate called Boia who, according to legend, terrorised the neighbourhood before being converted by St David.

At the end of the farm buildings, turn right along another track, which soon bears left and continues, between hedgebanks, to a lane. Turn left along the lane, descending into a hollow and, just before a bridge, turn right **G** along a farm track to Felin Isaf (Old Bishop's

Mill). Cross a bridge over a stream, bear left in front of a house and head slightly uphill to go through a gate. Continue along a delightful, enclosed, grassy path above the shallow wooded valley of the River Alun, passing beneath an avenue of trees and gradually curving right to reach a lane.

Turn left towards St David's, take the right-hand road at the fork just ahead and continue uphill to the town centre where you keep straight ahead, along the High Street to return to the car park. ●

Bosherston Lily Ponds and the Green Bridge of Wales

		GPS waypoints
Start	Bosherston	
Distance	10 miles (16.1km). Shorter version 3½ miles (5.7km)	⬛ SR 967 948 Ⓐ SR 975 947 Ⓑ SR 976 935
Height gain	820 feet (250m). Shorter version 260 feet (80m)	Ⓒ SR 966 930 Ⓓ SR 925 946
Approximate time	5 hours (2 hours for shorter version)	
Parking	National Trust car park at Bosherston	
Route terrain	Clear paths through woodland and along clifftops. A short section of quiet road	
Ordnance Survey maps	Landranger 158 (Tenby & Pembroke), Explorer OL36 (South Pembrokeshire)	

From the village of Bosherston the walk follows the side of the lily ponds to the sandy beach at Broad Haven and continues via cliff tops to St Govan's Head and Chapel. Here the shorter version returns along the road to Bosherston, but if the coast path across the army range is open it is definitely worth continuing along the flat-topped limestone cliffs as far as the twin spectacular sights of the Elegug Stacks and the Green Bridge of Wales. From here the walk returns along the same route as far as St Govan's Chapel and continues by road back to Bosherston.

Occasionally the walk is not possible because the army range is closed. If the red flags are flying on the boundary of the range at point Ⓑ, firing is in progress and you cannot proceed any further, in which case retrace your steps by the side of the lily ponds to the start. To check if the army range is open, consult the notice-board outside the café in Bosherston or telephone local tourist information centres (Pembroke 01437 776499). While inside the range boundary it is most important that you follow the line of white marker-posts and heed the warnings posted at the entrances.

Although small and fairly remote, Bosherston is a good walking centre with its pub, **St Govan's Country Inn**, good parking facilities and easy access to some fine coastal scenery. It also has an interesting 13th-century church and the lily ponds.

⬛ Start by going down the steps at the bottom end of the car park and continue down to the ponds, now maintained by the National Trust, which provides a series of useful information boards. The ponds, formerly part of the vast Stackpole estate, are three arms of a lake artificially created in the 18th century by damming the creek. They form an attractive scenic feature, especially in early summer when the waterlilies are in bloom. Walk down the main path and turn right to cross a bridge. Turn right on the other side and continue around the pond until the path veers left and descends to another bridge. A detour to the right, just before the bridge, brings you to a commanding viewpoint.

Cross the bridge, turn right and walk to a footpath sign at a T-junction of tracks and turn right. At the next footpath sign, turn right over a third, wider, bridge Ⓐ and walk along a sandy track, alongside the edge of the dunes of Stackpole Warren. From here there are superb views to the right looking up the well-wooded shoreline of the ponds, and Bosherston church can just be seen on the skyline. At the end of the pond, bear right to a footpath sign and keep ahead, bearing right around the base of a cliff to cross a footbridge. Then bear left to walk across the glorious sandy beach of Broad Haven, following the edge of the dunes round to the right to reach some steps at the far end of the beach. Climb them and continue up to a footpath sign by a car park.

Turn left along the coast path, go through a gate and, with a good view of St Govan's Head in front, continue up to another gate at the entrance to the Castlemartin Military Firing Range Ⓑ.

At this point you will have to turn back and retrace your steps to the start if the range is closed. Otherwise keep ahead, following the line of white marker-posts along a clear track across the top

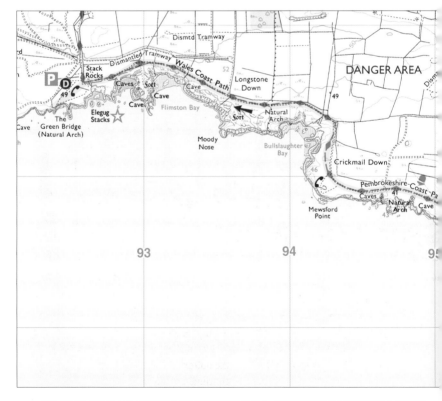

of the open, grassy, gorse-strewn cliffs, keeping more or less in a straight line and later picking up a tarmac path that leads to St Govan's car park **C**. To the left steps lead steeply down to the almost inaccessible St Govan's Chapel, lying at the foot of a narrow cleft in the rocks. This tiny 13th-century chapel, which measures only about 18 by 12 feet (5.5 by 3.6m), occupies the site of a hermit's cell allegedly founded in the 6th century by St Govan, a Celtic monk who chose the life of a hermit in this remote spot after enjoying the exalted rank of abbot in Ireland.

For the shorter version of the walk turn right at the car park and follow the lane back to Bosherston.

From the car park, keep ahead to go through a gate in another firing range boundary fence and continue along the coast path for just over 3 miles to Stack Rocks car park. For most of this section you walk along or beside a vehicle track, but after the track bends to the right keep ahead along a broad grassy track, taking care to follow the line of white marker-posts all the time. This is an easy and fairly flat walk, with extensive views to the right inland, and it passes some spectacular cliff scenery, particularly the narrow chasm of the Huntsman's Leap near the start and Bullslaughter Bay and the Elegug Stacks at the end.

On reaching the car park **D**, continue across the grass, and just in front of the boundary fence of the prohibited military zone a viewing platform gives a dramatic view of the great natural arch of the Green Bridge of Wales and the cliffs stretching beyond.

Both the Elegug Stacks and the Green

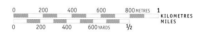

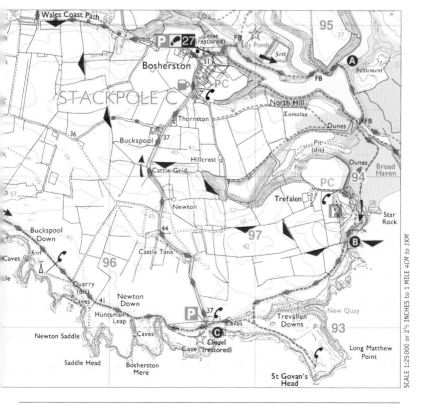

Bridge were formed through the action of sea water, salt, wind and rain wearing away the softer bands of limestone. The arch of the Green Bridge represents an early stage in the process; the final stage is when the roof of the arch collapses to leave a detached stack.

From here retrace your steps to St Govan's car park Ⓒ and turn left along the road for 1¼ miles to return to Bosherston. ⬤

The spectacular natural arch of the Green Bridge of Wales

The Preseli Ridge

		GPS waypoints
Start	Bwlch-gwynt, highest point on B4329 about halfway between Haverfordwest and Cardigan	SN 074 321
		A SN 081 323
Distance	10½ miles (16.9km). Shorter version 9½ miles (15.3km)	**B** SN 129 325
		C SN 144 325
Height gain	1,510 feet (460m). Shorter version 1,295 feet (395m)	**D** SN 065 320
Approximate time	5 hours (4½ hours for shorter version)	
Parking	Parking area just off road at Bwlch-gwynt	
Route terrain	Grassy and boggy paths, sometimes quite vague, over exposed hillsides. *Awkward navigation in poor visibility*	
Ordnance Survey maps	Landranger 145 (Cardigan & Mynydd Preseli), Explorer OL35 (North Pembrokeshire)	

This exhilarating ridge walk follows an ancient trackway, littered with prehistoric remains, across the wild, bare moorland of the Preseli Hills. The trackway was once part of a major route between England and Ireland. The splendid moorland walking and magnificent all-round views can be enjoyed for relatively little effort as the walk starts on the ridge itself at Bwlch-gwynt and goes along it as far as the prominent rocky outcrop of Carn Menyn before returning along the same route to the start. The track is undulating with no particularly steep or strenuous sections but it is likely to be muddy in places and at times becomes indistinct. Route finding is aided by a series of obvious rocky outcrops but because of this the walk should not be attempted in bad, especially misty, weather unless walkers are properly equipped for such conditions and experienced in using a compass. *The full walk continues from Bwlch-gwynt to the summit of Foel Eryr, an extra section worth while for the superb view over Cardigan Bay, the Gwaun Valley and Carningli.*

From the parking area keep beside the wire fence on the right, soon walking along the edge of the conifers of Pantmaenog Forest. Where the wire fence and forest edge both turn to the right, bear half-right **A** and head across the rough grassy moorland to cut a corner, soon rejoining the edge of the forest and bearing left to continue alongside it. Beyond the end of the conifers the track keeps ahead to the first landmark, the Bronze Age burial mound of Foel Feddau. To the right is Foel Cwmcerwyn, the highest point on

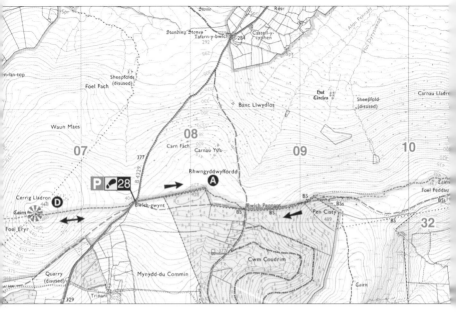

the Preselis (1,760 feet/536m).

The remainder of the walk has open and sweeping views as it follows the ridge. Keep ahead, descending gradually into a dip and passing to the left of the next landmark, the large, atmospheric group of dolerite rocks of Cerrigmarchogion, the 'rocks of the knights'. As you continue to descend, the next landmark can be seen on the skyline: the prominent pile of rocks called Carn Bica on the left flank of the hill in front. Start climbing gently and, on reaching a line of posts, bear right at a fork in the track to follow these posts to Carn Bica, another Bronze Age burial mound **B**. Pass to the right of these rocks, and a few yards ahead is a small circle of stones, possibly a neolithic burial chamber but named Beddarthur after the legendary warrior king, one of his numerous alleged resting places throughout Wales and south-west England.

Ahead is the great conical-shaped hill of Foeldrygarn and to the right is Carn Menyn, a particularly large group of rocks that dominates the skyline. Follow a path that heads downhill and up again to these rocks across what is now more heathery moorland. The path is not always clear, but bear slightly right and simply head towards the rocks **C**; immediately beyond them is a conifer plantation. Carn Menyn is the largest and most spectacular of the many outcrops of dolerite rocks on the Preselis and is one of the supposed sources of the smaller circle of bluestones found at Stonehenge. Why stones from here were used in the construction of Stonehenge and how they were transported there are among the greatest mysteries of prehistory. Some allege that they were carried by human effort and some claim that they were moved as a result of glacial action. It is unlikely that Carn Menyn was ever a quarry; the massive rocks have been shattered by the action of the weather rather than the work of man. But stones identical to the ones here and likely to have been found in this vicinity were certainly used at Stonehenge.

After exploring Carn Menyn retrace your steps to the start; from this

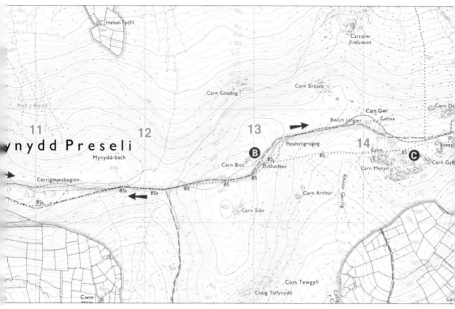

SCALE 1:33333 or 2 INCHES to 1 MILE 3CM to 1KM

| 0 | 200 | 400 | 600 | 800 METRES | 1 |
| 0 | 200 | 400 | 600 YARDS | ½ | |

KILOMETRES
MILES

direction there are some particularly
outstanding views of Foel Cwmcerwyn,
Carningli and the coast.

*The shorter version of the walk
finishes at Bwlch-gwynt.*

To see the magnificent view from
Foel Eryr, cross the road at Bwlchgwynt

and follow the clear grassy path ahead
up to the 1,535 feet (467m) summit **D**,
which is marked by a burial cairn
and a national park view indicator,
which points out Carningli, Dinas
Island, the Gwaun Valley and, peeping
above the conifers, the summit of Foel
Cwmcerwyn.   ●

The Preseli Ridge

Further Information

Safety on the Hills

The hills, mountains and moorlands of Britain, though of modest height compared with those in many other countries, need to be treated with respect. Friendly and inviting in good weather, they can quickly be transformed into wet, misty, windswept and potentially dangerous areas of wilderness in bad weather. Even on an outwardly fine and settled summer day, conditions can rapidly deteriorate at high altitudes and, in winter, even more so.

Therefore it is advisable to always take both warm and waterproof clothing, sufficient nourishing food, a hot drink, first-aid kit, torch and whistle. Wear suitable footwear, such as strong walking boots or shoes that give a good grip over rocky terrain and on slippery slopes. Try to obtain a local weather forecast and bear it in mind before you start. Do not be afraid to abandon your proposed route and return to your starting point in the event of a sudden and unexpected deterioration in the weather. Do not go alone and allow enough time to finish the walk well before nightfall.

Most of the walks described in this book do not venture into remote wilderness areas and will be safe to do, given due care and respect, at any time of year in all but the most unreasonable weather. Indeed, a crisp, fine winter day often provides perfect walking conditions, with firm ground underfoot and a clarity that is not possible to achieve in the other seasons of the year. A few walks, however, are suitable only for reasonably fit and experienced hill walkers able to use a compass and should definitely not be tackled by anyone else during the winter months or in bad weather, especially high winds and mist. These are indicated in the general description that precedes each of the walks.

Walkers and the Law

The Countryside and Rights of Way Act (CRoW Act 2000) extends the rights of access previously enjoyed by walkers in England and Wales. Implementation of these rights began on 19 September 2004. The Act amends existing legislation and for the first time provides access on foot to certain types of land – defined as mountain, moor, heath, down and registered common land.

Where You Can Go
Rights of Way
Prior to the introduction of the CRoW Act, walkers could only legally access the countryside along public rights of way. These are either 'footpaths' (for walkers only) or 'bridleways' (for walkers, riders on horseback and pedal cyclists). A third category called 'Byways open to all traffic' (BOATs), is used by motorised vehicles as well as those using non-mechanised transport. Mainly they are green lanes, farm and estate roads, although occasionally they will be found crossing mountainous area.

Rights of way are marked on Ordnance Survey maps. Look for the green broken lines on the Explorer maps, or the red dashed lines on Landranger maps.

The term 'right of way' means exactly what it says. It gives a right of passage over what, for the most part, is private land. Under pre-CRoW legislation walkers were required to keep to the line of the right of way and not stray onto land on either side. If you did inadvertently wander off the right of way, either because of faulty map reading or because the route was not clearly indicated on the ground, you were technically trespassing.

Local authorities have a legal obligation to ensure that rights of way are kept clear and free of obstruction, and are signposted where they leave metalled roads. The duty of local authorities to install signposts

Countryside Access Charter

Your rights of way are:

- public footpaths – on foot only. Sometimes waymarked in yellow
- bridle-ways – on foot, horseback and pedal cycle. Sometimes waymarked in blue
- byways (usually old roads), most 'roads used as public paths' and, of course, public roads – all traffic has the right of way

Use maps, signs and waymarks to check rights of way. Ordnance Survey Explorer and Landranger maps show most public rights of way

On rights of way you can:

- take a pram, pushchair or wheelchair if practicable
- take a dog (on a lead or under close control)
- take a short route round an illegal obstruction or remove it sufficiently to get past

You have a right to go for recreation to:

- public parks and open spaces – on foot
- most commons near older towns and cities – on foot and sometimes on horseback
- private land where the owner has a formal agreement with the local authority

In addition you can use the following by local or established custom or consent, but ask for advice if you are unsure:

- many areas of open country, such as moorland, fell and coastal areas, especially those in the care of the National Trust, and some commons
- some woods and forests, especially those owned by the Forestry Commission
- country parks and picnic sites
- most beaches
- canal towpaths
- some private paths and tracks Consent sometimes extends to horse-riding and cycling

For your information:

- county councils and London boroughs maintain and record rights of way, and register commons
- obstructions, dangerous animals, harassment and misleading signs on rights of way are illegal and you should report them to the county council
- paths across fields can be ploughed, but must normally be reinstated within two weeks
- landowners can require you to leave land to which you have no right of access
- motor vehicles are normally permitted only on roads, byways and some 'roads used as public paths'

extends to the placing of signs along a path or way, but only where the authority considers it necessary to have a signpost or waymark to assist persons unfamiliar with the locality.

The New Access Rights
Access Land

As well as being able to walk on existing rights of way, under the new legislation you now have access to large areas of open land. You can of course continue to use rights of way footpaths to cross this land, but the main difference is that you can now lawfully leave the path and wander at will, but only in areas designated as access land.

Where to Walk

Areas now covered by the new access rights – Access Land – are shown on Ordnance Survey Explorer maps by a light yellow tint surrounded by a pale orange border. New orange coloured 'i' symbols on the maps will show the location of permanent access information boards installed by the access authorities.

Restrictions

The right to walk on access land may lawfully be restricted by landowners. Landowners can, for any reason, restrict access for up to 28 days in any year. They cannot however close the land:

- on bank holidays;
- for more than four Saturdays and Sundays in a year;
- on any Saturday from 1 June to 11 August; or

- on any Sunday from 1 June to the end of September.

They have to provide local authorities with five working days' notice before the date of closure unless the land involved is an area of less than five hectares or the closure is for less than four hours. In these cases landowners only need to provide two hours' notice.

Whatever restrictions are put into place on access land they have no effect on existing rights of way, and you can continue to walk on them.

Dogs

Dogs can be taken on access land, but must be kept on leads of two metres or less between 1 March and 31 July, and at all times where they are near livestock. In addition landowners may impose a ban on all dogs from fields where lambing takes place for up to six weeks in any year. Dogs may be banned from moorland used for grouse shooting and breeding for up to five years.

In the main, walkers following the routes in this book will continue to follow existing rights of way, but a knowledge and understanding of the law as it affects walkers, plus the ability to distinguish access land marked on the maps, will enable anyone who wishes to depart from paths that cross access land either to take a shortcut, to enjoy a view or to explore.

General Obstructions

Obstructions can sometimes cause a problem on a walk and the most common of these is where the path across a field has been ploughed over. It is legal for a farmer to plough up a path provided that it is restored within two weeks. This does not always happen and you are faced with the dilemma of following the line of the path, even if this means treading on crops, or walking round the edge of the field. Although the latter course of action seems the most sensible, it does mean that you would be trespassing.

Other obstructions can vary from overhanging vegetation to wire fences across the path, locked gates or even a cattle feeder on the path.

Use common sense. If you can get round the obstruction without causing damage, do so. Otherwise only remove as much of the obstruction as is necessary to secure passage.

If the right of way is blocked and cannot be followed, there is a long-standing view that in such circumstances there is a right to deviate, but this cannot wholly be relied on. Although it is accepted in law that highways (and that includes rights of way) are for the public service, and if the usual track is impassable, it is for the general good that people should be entitled to pass into another line. However, this should not be taken as indicating a right to deviate whenever a way becomes impassable. If in doubt, retreat.

Report obstructions to the local authority and/or The Ramblers.

 Useful Organisations

Cadw (Welsh Historic Monuments)
Welsh Assembly Government,
Plas Carew, Unit 5/7 Cefn Coed,
Parc Nantgarw Cardiff CF15 7QQ
Tel. 01443 336000
www.cadw.gov.wales

Campaign for the Protection of Rural Wales
Tŷ Gwyn, 31 High Street,
Welshpool, Powys SY21 7YD
Tel. 01938 552525/556212
www.cprw.org.uk

Carmarthenshire County Council
County Hall, Carmarthen
SA31 1JP
Tel. 01267 234567
www.carmarthenshire.gov.wales

Campaign for National Parks
5-11 Lavington Street,
London, SE1 0NZ
Tel. 020 7981 0890
www.cnp.org.uk

Long Distance Walkers' Association
www.ldwa.org.uk

National Trust
Membership and general enquiries:
Tel. 0344 800 1895
www.nationaltrust.org.uk
Wales Regional Office
Priest House, Tredegar House,
Newport NP10 8YW
Tel. 01633 811659

Natural Resources Wales
Tŷ Cambria, 29 Newport Road,
Cardiff, CF24 0TP
Tel. 0300 065 3000
www.naturalresourceswales.gov.uk

Ordnance Survey
Tel. 03456 050 505 (Lo-call)
www.ordnancesurvey.co.uk

Pembrokeshire Coast National Park
Llanion Park,
Pembroke Dock,
Pembrokeshire,
SA72 6DY
Tel. 01646 624800
www.pembrokeshirecoast.org.uk
Information Centres:
St David's Tel. 01437 720392
Newport Tel. 01239 820912
Tenby Tel. 01834 845040

Pembrokeshire County Council
County Hall, Haverfordwest
SA61 1TP
Tel. 01437 764551
www.pembrokeshire.gov.uk

Ramblers
Main office: 2nd Floor, Camelford House,
87–90 Albert Embankment,
London SE1 7TW
Tel. 020 7339 8500
Wales: 3 Coopers Yard,
Curran Road,
Cardiff CF10 5NB
Tel. 0292064 4308
www.ramblers.org.uk

Tourist Information
www.visitcarmarthenshire.co.uk
www.visitpembrokeshire.com

Local tourist information offices
Cardigan: 01239 613230
Carmarthen: 01267 231557
Fishguard: 01437 776636
Haverfordwest: 01437 763110
Llandovery: 01550 720693
Milford Haven: 01437 771888
National Botanic Gardens: 01588 667149
Pembroke: 01437 776499
St David's: 01437 720392
Saundersfoot: 01834 813672
Tenby: 01437 775603

Youth Hostels Association
Trevelyan House, Dimple Road,
Matlock, Derbyshire DE4 3YH
Tel. 01629 592700
www.yha.org.uk

 ## Ordnance Survey maps of Pembrokeshire and Carmarthenshire

Pembrokeshire and Carmarthenshire are covered by Ordnance Survey 1:50 000 scale (1¼ inches to 1 mile or 2cm to 1km) Landranger map sheets 145, 157, 158 and 159.

To examine the area in more detail, and especially if you are planning walks, Explorer OL35 (North Pembrokeshire) and Explorer OL36 (South Pembrokeshire) at 1:25 000 scale (2½ inches to 1 mile or 4cm to 1km) are ideal.

The other maps that cover this guide are:
Explorer 177 (Carmarthen & Kidwelly)
Explorer 185 (Newcastle Emlyn)
Explorer 186 (Llandeilo & Brechfa Forest)

Ordnance Survey

Pathfinder® Guides — Britain's best-loved walking guides